TO WALK AND NOT FAINT

John,

Please accept this book as an expression of our gratitude for all that you have done to help us establish our home. Thanks for all your work — in moving us, in providing transportation for me, in assisting with so many little odd jobs — and for all your prayers and words of encouragement.

We pray that God would enfold you in His comfort and empower you with its joy! Deepest love & gratitude,

Norma & the EPHESUS community

TO WALK AND NOT FAINT

Marva Sedore

CHRISTIAN HERALD BOOKS
Chappaqua, New York 10514

to my parents,
whose model of ministry
gave direction and purpose
to my life

Library of Congress Cataloging in Publication Data

Sedore, Marva J.
    To walk and not faint.

    1. Bible. O.T. Isaiah XL — Meditations. I. Title
BS1520.S4   224′.106   80-65433
ISBN 0-915684-65-9

MEMBER OF
EVANGELICAL CHRISTIAN
PUBLISHERS ASSOCIATION

Christian Herald, independent, evangelical and interdenominational, is dedicated to publishing wholesome, inspirational and religious books for Christian families. "The books you can trust."

First Edition
CHRISTIAN HERALD BOOKS
40 Overlook Drive, Chappaqua, New York 10514
Printed in the United States of America

CONTENTS

Introduction

The thought struck me while I was swimming my usual mile to keep in shape. Suddenly I realized why Christians are so unusual. We are the only people who have the resources to face all of life. Our relationship with God and His revelation of Himself in His Word enable us to handle every dimension of our existence, from the personal frustrations of our private lives to the frightening threats of world war and economic chaos.

The realization made me want to cry out to everyone around me the good news of the hope and strength that are available to God's people. But most of the people around me in the pool were too caught up in the things of this world to care much about Jesus Christ and the life of faith. They needed first to hear the cries of the emptiness of this life, of the futility of life without God.

"A voice says, 'Cry!'" Isaiah recorded. "What shall I cry?" he responded, and the voice gave him a very important message to proclaim. As I studied this bit of dialogue in Isaiah 40, I was struck by the way the whole chapter deals with so many of the critical issues of life. In each verse I discovered a significant message for my life and a profound motivation for growth in my discipleship. It took me a whole month to think through that chapter and all it contains (and yet I feel I've only begun to scratch the surface of its treasures).

Oh, the changes that take place in our lives as we get to know God better! And each time I study intensely a verse from the

Scriptures, God's Word reveals to me so much more of Who He is. So I want to invite you to join me in getting to know God as He relates to all the cries of our existence, in realizing how our relationship with Him gives us the unusual ability to handle all the dimensions of life.

Before we begin these studies, however, we need both historical and theological background. The first thirty-nine chapters of the book of Isaiah are predominantly messages of warning and rebuke, and doom oracles pronounced against various nations, including the chosen people, the Jews. Occasionally, a song of Joy intrudes (notably chaps. 12 and 35), and many of the most significant prophecies concerning the Messiah (such as 7:14, 9:2-7, and 11:1-10) appear in this first part of the book. But the major mood of these thirty-nine chapters is denunciatory; the style is terse.

Suddenly, however, the mood and style change. After three historical chapters recording again the siege of Sennacherib in 701 B.C. and the illness of King Hezekiah (almost identical to the account in 2 Kings 18-20), the fortieth chapter of Isaiah shifts dramatically to intense poetry of awesome majesty and empowering comfort.

Because of this tremendous difference between the parts of the book, and because the second and third parts seem to reflect the historical background of the sixth century before Christ, it is commonly thought by many modern scholars that chapters 40 to 55 were written by a much more gifted poet after 538 B.C., or almost two hundred years after the time of the prophet Isaiah. Then, because the last eleven chapters describe a time after the restoration of the temple, many of those same scholars date chapters 56 to 66 from after 512 B.C.

Making chapters 40 to 66 the expression of poets living two hundred years later, however, is unnecessary to account for the changes in mood, style, and content in the book of Isaiah. For historical, literary, and theological reasons too numerous to detail here, I am convinced that the book has thematic and stylistic integrity. It was entirely the work of one writer, the prophet Isaiah.

We are not going to get involved in the technical issues that concern theologians and scholars. Instead, we want to get into an intensive study of only one chapter, with each meditation developed as follows: observing what the text says, interpreting those words to discover what they mean, and then applying the message to our lives. I trust not only that you will benefit from these particular meditations on Isaiah 40, but also that you will be equipped by this book to study the Scriptures in your own meditations on other passages.

The chief character of these pages is the LORD as He reveals Himself to His people. I have followed the customary practice in Bibles of putting the words LORD and GOD into capital letters when the Hebrew word to be translated is the name *Yahweh*. That is the name by which the LORD revealed Himself to Moses in Exodus 6:2-8. It is a term that distinguishes Him from all the neighboring, false deities; He is not just a god, but He alone is the great "I AM."

Throughout the Old Testament, the name *Yahweh*, the LORD, implies the faithfulness of GOD, especially as He delivers His people. We need to recover this image in our age, to learn the glory of the LORD's constant faithfulness to His covenant and His effective deliverance of His people from all their captivities.

It is also my peculiar custom to capitalize not only all nouns and pronouns that refer to God (such as He, Who, and so on), but also words that describe characteristics that I want the reader to recognize as coming directly from Him or from our relationship with Him (words such as *Truth* and *Joy*). That way the specific Joy of the LORD can be easily distinguished from mere (and fading) human happiness.

I pray that you might experience that Joy as you read the pages that follow and meditate on the stirring messages that we as God's people have to tell others. A voice keeps saying, "Cry!"

The Cry of Comfort 1

"Comfort, comfort my people, says your God."
Isaiah 40:1

Where in the world can you and I find comfort and help in the tough situations of life? Your husband suddenly seems so distant and drifting still further away. Or you just don't know what to do with a son or daughter who is becoming rebellious. Maybe you wonder why you can't get past the depression that seems to engulf you. Who will ease the stabbing tensions of our lives, or who can bring relief from the dull, throbbing ache of loneliness?

Perhaps despair is your constant companion. If you don't feel it now, you can remember times when you felt totally helpless. Possibly conversation ceased in your marriage, or a job got too hard. Perhaps you anticipate even more difficult times as your children grow up, as your work gets more competitive and hectic. At one time or another, we all feel so overwhelmed by our situations that we grope for any fragment of comfort to sustain us.

Yet where in the world can comfort be found?

Isaiah's time was no better. The Israelites were overcome with despair. They had lost sight of their purpose as the Chosen People. Intrigue and rebellion, hypocritical worship and injustice, materialism and idolatry of all sorts — the same sins plagued the people in Isaiah's time as plague the world today.

Suddenly, however, the fortieth chapter of Isaiah ushers in an entirely different mood. In the midst of the darkness of sin and despair, God commands the prophet to proclaim a message of light and hope. Similarly, in the midst of the troubled times of our personal lives, and into the shambles of twentieth century culture,

God calls to His people today to hear a new word, a word of comfort and victory.

"Comfort, comfort my people, says your God," the fortieth chapter begins. Each phrase of that short first verse brings a message of comfort.

"Comfort, comfort," God repeats to a nameless audience. One call to comfort is not enough, for pain and suffering are deep, and agony is long. The fact that the verb occurs twice implies that the comfort we are being offered is continuous. There IS comfort to be given, God declares.

The King James Version captures better the plural sense of this verb when it translates the imperative, "Comfort ye, comfort ye." (Perhaps a Southern version — "comfort y'all" — would capture its essence even better!) Isaiah was not the only one called to offer solace to those who grieve or doubt or fear. This verse reaches out of the pages of our Bibles to call you and me to the ministry of comforting. The repetition of the verb reminds us that our ministry can be continuous as well. There is plenty of comfort for us to receive and to give.

Not only is there a bounteous supply, but what we receive and give is truly comforting. The world offers its solace, but it has no substance. Its words are hypnotic, but they do not heal. The world would comfort us with false hopes or pretensions by feeding our egos or nursing our grudges. On the other hand, God wants to give us the comfort of His Truth, the entire Truth concerning our condition in relation to Him.

Several years ago when I became ill, some of my well-meaning friends offered me what I would call the world's comfort. They attempted to cheer me with such words as these: "It will be all right," or "A lot of people suffer severe illnesses," or "Soon you can go back to living a normal life."

The problem with such words is that they had no basis, no substance, no reality. Things may turn out all right, but at the moment, in a time of pain, it did not seem that way. Nor did the fact that others go through the same experience make it any easier for me in that moment of crisis. In fact, those statements made me feel all the more guilty; I knew I should trust God and thank Him and do other such good things. But the pain remained. I could not deny my feelings, and I couldn't silence my guilt about them. The final word of supposed comfort contradicted my doctor's advice and so discouraged me all the more.

On the other hand, the president of the congregation I was serving at the time offered this message of true comfort: "The LORD is with you, and I care." What a precious assurance! What a sweet comfort that was — to hear in the midst of pain and grief and guilt that God was there beside me, inside me, not condemning, to give me His everlasting solace! Words of comfort from a human perspective will pass away, but words about our eternal, unchanging, and caring Father will continue to abide and to offer comfort that endures and is true.

The second phrase of verse 1 emphasizes the intimacy of this comfort. God commands His listeners to comfort "*My* people." His comfort is effective and personal because He has chosen to make us His people. We are not left stranded in a confused world, torn by circumstances or adrift in a sea of meaninglessness. God has a particular interest in what happens to each of us. And not only does He care, but He also has the power to do something about it all.

God is sovereign! He really does love each one of us as very important individuals in His eternal plans. Therefore, we can know that no matter the circumstances, no matter even our frequent failures to trust Him, God wants to fill our lives with His deepest Joys.

We ARE His people. He has demonstrated that in the cross of His Son and sealed it with the gift of His Spirit. If we have been given these gifts of His grace, will He not also freely give us everything else we might need (Rom. 8:32)?

The third phrase of this first verse drives the point home. We are not called to offer comfort just because we feel like it, but, rather, because that is what the Lord says. God's revelation about Himself declares to us that He wants His people to be comforted. The phrase, "says your God," carries with it an immense authority. What God says, He will do. Consequently, when we seek to give His comfort to someone else, we can know that we are really giving it to him. It will indeed be available for him to receive. The Word of the Lord never comes back void, but always it accomplishes that purpose for which it was sent (Isa. 55:10-11).

The implications of these three phrases have a double application for our lives — one for ourselves and one for the way they affect our relationships with others. For ourselves, we can realize that God brings this word of consolation to us personally in whatever situations we might be confronting. Based on the authority of His Word and on the fact that He called us to be His own, we can be sure of His consolation in our trials, of His hope in our despair, of His peace in our confusion, and of His faithful presence in our bad times and good times.

For others, we have the capability, because of what we have learned from God, to offer deep and meaningful solace. We can assure them that God speaks graciously to His people continuously. When we meet people who need hope and assurance, we do not have to settle for sentimental drivel or pious platitudes. We can give them solid comfort, consolations that are genuine and eternal — and free, out of the richness of God's most abundant grace.

What kind of comfort do you offer to those who need to hear consolation? What do you say, for example, to the good friend whose parent just died, to the neighbor who lost his job, to your husband who was bypassed for a promotion?

What kind of comfort do you carry with you into the uncomfortable situations of your life? What sustains you when the church committee on which you serve isn't doing its job well, when you find yourself failing as a parent, when you realize that your wife doesn't really love you anymore? To you, also, this word is addressed: "Comfort, comfort my people, says your God."

QUESTIONS FOR FURTHER MEDITATION:

My words cannot take this verse from Isaiah 40 and apply it specifically to your life. I can't know what your particular needs and struggles might be. Therefore, I invite you to take a closer look at Isaiah 40:1 as it relates to your life by means of the following questions. Take time to ponder them; talk them over with your neighbor; discuss them in a Bible study group at your church or place of work. And I will be praying that you will find specific comfort and deep Joy in your relationship with God as you meditate upon His Word and get to know Him better.

1. How have I experienced the difference between the vain comfort the world gives and the everlastingly real comfort to be found in the Lord?

2. Why does the Word of God bear so much authority?

3. Why is it important to me that I, personally and individually, am one of God's people?

4. By what means can I offer God's comfort (rather than the world's) to my friends in need?

5. What kind of comfort does God have to offer in this mixed-up and frightening twentieth century culture, when war and nuclear destruction, famine, turmoil, and depersonalization threaten from every side?

6. What are some favorite Bible verses that give me special comfort in times of distress? (some examples: Lam. 3:22-33, Psalms 27 and 34, many of the discourses in the gospel of John, Rom. 8, 1 Pet. 5:6-11, Hab. 3:17-19, and, of course, the verses of Isa. 40).

7. What are some of the aspects of the character of God implied by this verse and my study of it, and how can the knowledge of these characteristics be comforting to me?

The Cry of Release 2

"Speak tenderly to Jerusalem,
and cry to her
that her warfare is ended,
that her iniquity is pardoned,
that she has received from the LORD's hand
double for all her sins."

Isaiah 40:2

She moaned in pain and tried to move to a comfortable position. Paralysis from strokes confined her to a bed, and too many years in bed had given her terrible sores. Day after day as I visited her, I groped for something to say and agonized because there was nothing I could do to ease her suffering. I couldn't even touch her gently, because her weakness made it necessary that her visitors wear gowns and gloves. I could only touch her tenderly with my words. Finally, she broke her hip, and soon thereafter she died. At last she was out of pain. Now she could hear clearly the tender words of God Himself.

"Speak tenderly," verse 2 begins. The original Hebrew actually means, "Speak to the heart." Isn't it your heart that needs to be touched when you are hurting? Sometimes anguish wells up so powerfully, the pain seems so overwhelming, that we're sure it will break our hearts with grief. The one we love the most deceives us, or a goal toward which we've been groping in a long struggle proves unattainable in the end. The moments of crisis pass away, but what can we do with the mounds of pain that remain as a knot in our stomach? Who can comfort the aching of our agonies? "Speak to the heart of Jerusalem," God says.

Although the Children of Israel were a rebellious people, although it was because of their sin that they were to be taken away by the Babylonians into captivity, and although they repeatedly ignored the rebuke and warning of the prophet Isaiah, yet the LORD commands, "Speak tenderly to Jerusalem." They would need words of hope for their return, promises for encouragement in the future. The message of kindness that was to be called out is composed of these three bits of encouragement: that their term of service was over, that their sins had been forgiven, and that they had been punished enough.

Verse 1 commanded the listener to "comfort My people." Now verse 2 adds the verbs "speak to the heart" and "call out" to complete the three-part command. Then the rest of verse 2 describes the comforting message that is to be spoken kindly to the despairing people. These three verbs are a good summary of our ministries in our times, for often we offer comfort to others by speaking kindly to them or declaring to them the good news of grace.

To "speak to the heart" implies sensitivity and tenderness, laying a message close to the heart of another. The message about to be delivered is one of love; its grace uplifts. It is to be given with soothing gentleness and tender care. It is the message needed for the hour. How appropriately God's words are given to His people to meet their deepest hurts and needs!

Last Sunday was one of those precious days when the LORD spoke to my heart. I was recovering from oral surgery and was also saddened by the death of a dear friend. Burdens seemed to be too great to bear. Then, by a strange quirk of scheduling due to the opportunity to sing with a friend who plays the organ for another church, I had the privilege of hearing three different sermons in the morning. All three pastors spoke on this gospel text for the day: "Come unto me, all ye that labour and are heavy laden, and I will give you rest" (Matt. 11:28, KJV). From three different perspectives, and with my own meditation adding a fourth, I heard God's comforting Word spoken tenderly to my heart.

The number three was used by the Hebrew people to symbolize spiritual things. How much more clearly we New Testament people can understand that symbolic significance of three, for God has specifically revealed Himself to us as a trinity. In this second verse of Isaiah 40, two sets of three intensify the importance of God's message. First we are given three commands — "comfort," "speak to the heart," and "call out." Then we are told three special gifts of grace about which we should cry out. It saddens me to realize how often these dimensions of grace are missed in contemporary Christianity. We need to hear more clearly in our times this message with its special emphasis, reinforced by the doubling of threes.

First, we are told that the warfare of the people of God is over. In Isaiah's time, this primarily promised a physical end to the long, hard term of captive service. But, as the prophets who wrote after the exile show, this message was very much needed also for the struggles of the heart and spirit. Furthermore, this tremendous news prefigures the even greater news of Good Friday, when Jesus cried triumphantly from the cross that the warfare had been ended. He brought to the finish the fight against the devil and all the powers of sin and death. Then He arose, ascended, and sent the Holy Spirit to carry that victory into the lives of His people. Indeed, the warfare ended once and for all when Satan was eternally and unalterably defeated at Calvary.

Far too often, however, too many of God's people live as if the war still needed to be fought, as if the victory weren't already decided. Thinking we need to defeat the devil and his lies again from the beginning, we work and fight to win God's grace and favor. How desperately we need to hear the exultant cry that the warfare is ended! We Christians should constantly realize afresh the significance of that cry — that God has made it possible for us to rest in Him.

Of course, that does not mean we are not actively involved in living out our Christian commitment. Here we are dealing, however, with the strange paradox of the Christian life, namely, that we are actively involved in following Christ, but that it is the Spirit within us Who makes that following possible and carries it out.

Our own iniquity is one of the greatest barriers to following the Lord. That barrier is smashed, however, by the second of the three proclamations to be called out to Jerusalem, namely, that her iniquity has been removed. Her guilt has been pardoned because the punishment has been accepted as satisfactory. We in New Testament times know better how that can be true, for we know that Christ bore the punishment for us.

There is tremendous freedom in knowing that our iniquity has been pardoned. Our failures having been forgiven, we can begin to put into effect these words from Paul: "Forgetting what lies behind and straining forward to what lies ahead, I press on" (Phil. 3:13*b*-14*a*). Yet how much of our behavior is the result of guilt feelings? It is easy to get caught in a downward cycle of mistaken action or undesirable behavior, which causes us to feel more guilty, which causes us to respond even more poorly, which causes us to feel even more guilty, and so on.

One of my best friends struggles constantly with the agony of such a downward cycle. He is an extremely gifted young pianist who has had much trouble forcing himself to practice. Then he feels so guilty about his failures that his work sessions don't go well, which makes it all the more difficult for him to motivate himself to keep up the disciplines he knows are necessary. The consequence is a heavier burden of guilt.

The only way that such a downward cycle can be reversed is if it is stopped short. Isaiah's message of comfort is just such a cycle-stopper. Iniquity has been removed! God's child is freed by that news to begin moving in an upward cycle, rejoicing in forgiveness and working well because of the freedom of spirit that God's gracious forgiveness produces. What a cycle of Joy is attainable when the message of forgiveness is believed and lived upon!

The final proclamation of the three messages of good news to be cried out to Jerusalem concerns her suffering. It has been enough. The Hebrew word usually translated "received" in our versions is otherwise rendered "taken." The implication is that Israel has been actively involved in her own punishment. But now she has been amply punished. The verse seems to end expectantly. We eagerly await what will happen next — and are quickly greeted with the new call to prepare for the revealing of the glory of the LORD.

Three distinct periods mark the fulfillment of this verse. How much it must have meant to the Children of Israel as they waited in captivity for the punishment to be amply fulfilled! The faithful must have clung to this precious promise from Isaiah in the long years of looking forward to the day of their return from Babylon.

Second, all creation waited as Jesus hung on the cross until He had taken all the punishment we deserve. When everything necessary had been accomplished, He cried victoriously, "It has been brought to the finish!" Finally, because He has borne the punishment for us all, we can prepare for His coming again, the final revelation of God's people. This final waiting, surely, is the easiest, for we know already the ultimate outcome. The ending of our chastisement has been assured by Christ's victory over sin and death.

There doesn't have to be any doubt. The warfare is ended, the guilt is removed, the punishment is sufficient. What good news to speak tenderly to someone's heart!

QUESTIONS FOR FURTHER MEDITATION:

1. How might I learn to speak more tenderly to those in pain?
2. What kinds of warfare continue to engage my energies?
3. How could I learn to experience more thoroughly the victory over struggles, the ending of the term of hard service that Christ makes available to me?
4. What sources of guilt could I give over to the Lord, Who has sufficiently paid the price of pardon?
5. What is the meaning and place of chastisement in the Christian life?
6. How might I help someone overcome the cycles of guilt and despair?
7. How could I stir up in myself and others a greater anticipation of the events to follow these declarations of grace and forgiveness (see the comments on the following verse)?

The Cry to Prepare 3

"A voice cries:
'In the wilderness prepare the way of the LORD,
make straight in the desert a highway for our God.'"
Isaiah 40:3

It took all day. My good friend had been kidding me by answering, "Baked Alaska," every time I asked him what he wanted to eat. So for his birthday I had decided to make one. I invited several friends, baked the cake and froze it, shaped the ice cream and unmolded it on top of the cake, and prepared the egg whites for the meringue. In the last moments the ice cream and cake were sealed inside a shell of meringue, and the whole tray was put into a 500 degree oven. It worked! When we cut the slices of Baked Alaska, the meringue was nicely browned, and the ice cream was still frozen. I was delighted. All the preparations had been worthwhile. The happiness of the "unveiling" was worth the effort.

Far more worthwhile will be the joy of the unveiling anticipated by this verse. After the promise of the first two verses, Isaiah 40 continues with the command to prepare. The comfort that is coming is so good that we need to be stirred up to get ready to receive it. The preparations will be tremendously worthwhile, for the glory of the LORD Himself is going to be revealed (see v. 5).

John the Baptizer applied this verse to himself when he announced the coming of Jesus Christ. Describing the function of his preaching, he declared himself to be the one designated to prepare the way of the LORD. He was the fulfillment of this verse in the first sense. But a second sense of fulfillment applies to us. In our time we, too, are to be preparers.

The phrase that begins this verse actually means, "A voice is

23

heard calling." In verse 2 this same Hebrew verb occurred in the imperative form, "cry out." Now it occurs in the form of a participle to indicate that a voice making a proclamation keeps continuing to be heard. We don't have to speculate upon whose voice it is or where it comes from. We only need to know that the voice is heard, and the proclamation that it declares is that whoever listens should clear the way for the LORD. The prophet Isaiah, the Children of Israel, John the Baptizer, and we Christians today should make smooth in the desert a highway for our God.

How do we prepare in the wilderness a way for Yahweh? How do we make straight a highway for our God? The second Hebrew verb in the voice's command is intensive: "cause to be straight." There is definitely something that can be done by those who hear the voice to cause the way to be straight in preparation for Yahweh.

Above all, this verse applies to the attitudes of each person's heart. The way was prepared for Jesus to come the first time when John the Baptizer stirred up men's hearts to long for the Kingdom of God. Gloriously, when Jesus physically comes the second time, the way will be prepared for Him by angels and trumpets and all the hosts of heaven, but we don't know the day or the hour when that will occur. How do we make straight the way for our God to come to us now? How can we prepare in the wilderness a highway for the LORD?

I don't think it does violence to this text to apply it to our lives allegorically. Its graphic imagery challenged the Israelites to remove those obstructions that stood in the way and prevented the LORD's coming. Similarly, the wilderness might picture the barren stoniness of our hearts. This figure suggests the driest desert, windswept and without water, an apt characterization of a life without the LORD. To that emptiness our LORD Jesus Christ would come, bringing us streams of living water (John 7:38).

It's not that we could work to deserve His coming. It's not that by our efforts we make that coming possible. The problem is that He wants to come more richly into our lives, but is often prevented by the obstructions we keep building or by our failure to make smooth the way.

What kinds of things are obstructing His way? For some, the path is blocked by fears; for others, by pride or our own illusions,

illusions of our own importance, deceptive opinions of our own ability to handle things by ourselves.

Several years ago I visited the wilderness of Judea. I was astounded by its bleakness and desolation. I saw in that wilderness the terror of shifting sands. They moved with the winds and covered the highway. They blinded my eyes and stung my skin.

That is the problem of the wilderness about which Isaiah speaks. Our own hearts are seas of shifting sands. The winds of time and change blow everything all around and obstruct the highways that are there. We have to come to the conclusion that we are incapable of making a highway for our God. What can we do then? How can this task be fulfilled?

The message of the voice that cries is a stark reminder of our absolute need for God to do all things through us. We can't prepare a way for Him except by His grace. We can't clean out the obstructions; we can't make the way smooth except that He does it in us and through us. This third verse calls us to our knees in humble repentance, and it calls us to adoration, as we thank Him for His grace given so abundantly to work for us, in spite of us.

John the Baptizer knew that this was the way to fulfill the call to prepare. His entire task in life was to urge people to repent in order to receive the forgiveness of sins. That is how he prepared the way for the LORD to come. When Jesus arrived, John had accomplished his task.

Similarly, this verse calls us to repentance, and we, in turn, can invite others to repentance also. We as a Christian body need to be reminding each other of the need for constant preparation in the wilderness of our lives. Daily we need to recognize and repent of the obstructions we put there. It is the LORD Who wants to come and Who will enable us to prepare the way.

The implications of this verse take us one step further, however. We must realize that not only do we allow things to block His coming, but also, neglecting our hearts, we let them get scorched and made dry and barren. Our hearts have become a wilderness because they have not been cultivated. In the desert of our desperate and empty lives, we are called to prepare the way for the LORD. The cry to make a highway for our God to come invites us to the disciplines of cultivation — nourishing our hearts with God's Word, watering the stoniness with His gifts of Himself.

There can be no other response to this verse than for us to have a greater desire to make the way open. God is ready and waiting to come more richly into our lives. The way can be made more open by our spending time with Him, listening to His Word, hearing this voice calling and proclaiming to us that a way should be made, meditating, spending time in prayer, and hearing the calls of other members of His Kingdom. Our discipline cannot earn us His presence, but our discipline is a means by which the way can be cultivated.

This, too, is all made possible by His grace. Nothing can be done except as He draws us. No hunger can be stirred up in our hearts unless He stirs it up. So the voice urges us to prepare the way for the LORD. We are invited to join the ranks of the prophet Isaiah, John the Baptizer, and the seventy whom Jesus sent out two by two to prepare the way in all the cities to which He Himself was about to go (Luke 10). We are sent by this verse to prepare these places to which Jesus would come: into our own hearts and into the hearts of others.

QUESTIONS FOR FURTHER MEDITATION:
1. How can I hear the voice calling yet today?
2. What sins have I allowed to obstruct the way of the LORD's coming more deeply into my life?
3. What kinds of action cause the sands to shift and obstruct the highway?
4. How can I cultivate the wildernesses of my own life?
5. How can I help others to remove obstructions or to cultivate?
6. What do I desire to have growing in my former wildernesses?
7. What will it mean to me if God comes more fully into my life?

The Cry for Readiness 4

"Every valley shall be lifted up,
and every mountain and hill be made low;
the uneven ground shall become level,
and the rough places a plain."

Isaiah 40:4

I felt as if I were drowning in discouragement. In a time of great transition in my life, I was not sure how to sort through the criticism so that I could discard what didn't apply and be changed by what was valid. So I felt guilty about it all and had trouble finding much worth in myself.

Then I went to a meeting in San Diego, and a former student of mine drove with his fiancée all the way from Pasadena in the midst of a gas crisis to see me. His comments were so uplifting as he expressed deep appreciation of my ministry, which I had been questioning. Indeed, the valley of discouragement I'd been in was quickly lifted up.

An enormous lifting up is proclaimed in Isaiah 40:4, but it offers a strange geographical picture on which to meditate. What can be the purpose of lifting up the valleys and bringing down the high places? Following after the command to prepare the highway for our God in verse 3, this verse asks for some pretty tricky engineering. Why does faith have to move mountains, anyway?

We need a geography lesson to answer these questions. If we understand the topography that Isaiah describes as his listeners understood it, we can comprehend the voice's message to them as well as to us. We can look beneath the pictures of the land to see the powerful theology that underlies them. The voice is calling us to continue clearing out the obstructions that prevent God's coming. Two distinct operations are pictured in verse 4, each one accentuated by a poetic parallel.

The first two lines of the verse announce the lifting up of the low places and the bringing down of the high. The first verb is very picturesque; it actually shows the valleys coming up out of themselves, being pushed up to a position of exaltation. The same verb is used in Ruth 1:9 to describe Naomi's daughters-in-law lifting up their voices in weeping over the agony of separation.

While the valleys are being lifted, the mountains and high places are being brought down. The Hebrew word used here to designate those "high places" is used in other verses in the Old Testament to name the location of the altars at which the Israelites worshiped false gods. Perhaps this declaration that the high places shall be made low implies that those sanctuaries for idol worship would be destroyed.

These phrases speak about God as the great equalizer. When we think of valleys being lifted up and mountains being made low, we are reminded of the words of Mary in her Magnificat as she spoke of the poor being exalted and the rich being sent empty away (Luke 1:52-53).

Perhaps as we look at the countryside around Jerusalem, we can visualize what it would be like if the valleys and mountains were all made equal in preparation for the return of Christ. We can contemplate what it meant in Isaiah's time as a prophecy of the Old Testament preparation for the return from captivity. But what does this picture say to our lives now?

The first two phrases bring a strongly critical word to a society, such as ours, that promotes inequality. Of course, we proclaim that all men are created equal, and we march for equal rights, and we assert that all people have equal opportunity. Unfortunately, however, the reality of our society does not conform to that ideal. We see instead that certain attributes are given more honor than others. For example, in the university setting, those who earn more grant money are often more important than those who concentrate on teaching well. Often in the world of commerce, shrewdness is praised; the best tax evader receives the greatest respect from his peers. In high society, one who is beautiful or cultured or charming, the one who knows the right things or people, is worthy to be in the "in crowd." Everything becomes competitive.

Usually the result of this kind of society is that each person must strive to show himself worthy in some dimension. Individuals must prove to the world that they make important contributions. Everyone must assert himself to be the best in some way. The value of excellence is falsely elevated, and the result is a fanatic self-seeking and an idolatrous sense of superiority. To that kind of competitive striving, this verse speaks powerfully of a whole new order.

The freedom of the gospel for me is that as we prepare for the coming of the LORD, as we receive Him more thoroughly into our lives, and as we look to the day when He will come again, we no longer need to elevate ourselves to prove our worthiness. Instead, ours is a unique opportunity as God's people to usher in the truth of equality, for our worthiness lies in the fact that God has chosen us as His own.

What might be our task, then, in response to the voice that is heard making this proclamation? Perhaps our function is to lift up those who find themselves engulfed in sorrow, those swallowed by the valleys. Perhaps our function is to be a prophet, to call down those who have elevated themselves to positions on the mountains or those who are engaged in false worship on the idolatrous high places.

In each of these functions, the result is that each person is brought to the same realization that God will come to us only if the way before Him is prepared. Those in the valleys, those convinced of their worthlessness, are not in any position to receive the acceptance and love of God. It is true, to be sure, that God's acceptance of them lifts them up from the valleys. Those overwhelmed by their sin or grief, however, need to be prepared for a better understandng of God's grace.

On the other hand, those with confidence in themselves, those who are elevated on the mountains, need to be brought to recognize their unworthiness before the majesty of the great and holy God. They need to recognize the idolatry of their worship of self when they think they have reached the high places.

Not only does all of this apply to our relationships with other people in our ministry to them, but it also says some tremendous things to us personally. In our times of discouragement, we can claim the promise that we shall indeed be lifted up. On the other hand, in times of pride, in times of self-satisfaction, in times when we lose sight of the fact that God is the One Who accomplishes things through us, we must hear the call to be brought low. In both cases, the way of the LORD needs to be prepared in our lives.

The second set of two phrases in this verse speaks of openness and leveling, with the implication perhaps of productivity. "That which is crooked" at the beginning of the first phrase is a noun based on the same root from which the name Jacob (the "deceptive" or "crooked" one) is derived. Places so characterized shall become, the voice cries, as the *mishor*, which is a geographical term used in the Scriptures for two distinct places. It could mean either the Philistine plain around Gath and Gaza (the flat tableland west of Hebron) or the tableland east of the Dead Sea and south of the city of Amman. In both cases, the open plain is a profound contrast to that which is crooked. (You might want to look up those places on a map of Bible lands.)

The poetic parallel of the second phrase asserts that the rugged terrain shall become the *bukeah*, which is a little valley in the Judean wilderness on the north edge of the Dead Sea. Archaeological excavations in this area have shown that in the time of Uzziah (in the year of whose death Isaiah was called to be a prophet), the *bukeah* was developed into a farming, military settlement. The rocks of the land were cleared and used to channel the moisture down from the hillsides and to dam the edges of the fields so that, in the midst of a relatively dry area, the *bukeah* became a series of terraced fields outlined in stone. In other words, the rough places will become garden spots.

Both of these phrases seem to imply that the land that was untillable becomes usable. Consequently, this second half of verse 4 reminds me of Jesus' parable of the sowing of the seeds, in which those that fall into the good ground produce thirty-, sixty-, and one hundred-fold. Soon verse 5 will declare that the glory of the LORD will be revealed. These phrases suggest that as the ground of our hearts is prepared, it is made ready to be productive and fertile to bear that glory. The LORD uses the very stones of our lives to channel water for growth.

Again, there are implications both for our ministry and for our own lives. Perhaps our function is to straighten crooked or distorted understandings of God so that others' hearts are prepared to receive Him. Perhaps our function is to tear away the rough places, to remove the rocky parts that prohibit lush growth. Our personal need might be to receive God's polishing so that our rough edges might be worn down to make us more open to His coming.

I am grateful for the ministry of special friends who have constructively criticized me and so have knocked off some of my rocky edges. I think, for example, of Doug, who gently pointed out my lack of sensitivity, and of Joanie, who told me I was being a hypocrite and lambasted my false piety. I needed their rebukes and continue to need challenges to change.

The promise of the voice is that the crooked in us shall become as the *mishor*, and the rough places, the *bukeah*. Our mountains shall be brought down, and our low places exalted.

Our geography lesson is complete. Now perhaps the bulldozers better get to work. We've got a lot of earth to move.

QUESTIONS FOR FURTHER MEDITATION:

1. What attributes of my personality stand most in need of the preparation of this verse?

2. What does God use to lift me up from my valleys, and what does He use to bring me down from my high places?

3. How can I be a means for lifting others up?

4. What does it mean to be a prophet in this time?

5. How can I be a constructive and gentle prophet in helping others to come down from pretentious heights?

6. How can I make rough places more level and fertile, both in myself and in others?

7. How can I contribute to straightening the confusion and distortions of contemporary theological controversy?

The Cry of Revelation 5

"And the glory of the LORD shall be revealed,
and all flesh shall see it together,
for the mouth of the LORD has spoken."
Isaiah 40:5

First we were too high, and the clouds below our plane hid it from sight. Much later, after we'd landed, the clouds above blocked it from view. Even when we were at the right level, I couldn't see it for a while — the plane's wings were in the way. But finally all obstructions were cleared away, and there it was: Mount Rainier towering majestically in all its snowy glory. It was an incredibly beautiful sight, never to be forgotten. My ecstasy at the first moment of seeing it was heightened by the time of waiting and preparation. I anticipated a vision of one of the most beautiful mountains in all the world, and I was not disappointed.

Similarly, we are filled with anticipation as we undertake the preparations described in verse 4 of Isaiah 40. Will what we see be worth its price? What will be the result in our lives when our valleys are lifted up? What will we see when our mountains and hills are made low? What changes will occur when our uneven ground is leveled and the rough places are made into a plain? The result, the voice proclaims, is that the glory of the LORD shall be revealed, and all flesh shall see it together.

In the day when Isaiah recorded the voice's message, he spoke of the reestablishment of the temple and of the restoration of the people of Israel after the time of captivity in Babylon. The LORD's glory would be seen again in the promised land and, specifically, in His dwelling place, the temple.

Then, in the time of Jesus Christ, this message was partially fulfilled in the new temple of Jesus Himself, as He revealed God's glory in the signs He performed and took up His residence in the

33

lives of God's people. The verse anticipates the revealing of the glory of the LORD on Calvary and at the empty tomb. It prophesies such revealing of the LORD's glory as took place on Pentecost, when all flesh saw it together. But what does this verse say to our lives now?

A little Hebrew study makes the verse come alive for our times. The word *kabod*, which is translated "glory," means in its root "to be heavy," or "to make something important," or "weighty." Thus, the revealing of Yahweh's glory takes place when His importance is recognized, when His significant presence is made more fully known. Furthermore, that glorious revealing will be all the greater, verse 5 goes on to say, because all flesh shall see it together as one. All flesh, all mankind (the phrase perhaps even designates all creatures) will see it, with no doubt about it. God's revelation of Himself will be unmistakable.

The inevitability of that revelation is reinforced by the assertion, "For the mouth of the LORD has spoken." Both the noun phrase and the verb form are made more intensive by their construction in the original Hebrew. Consequently, they declare in no uncertain terms that Yahweh Himself has promised this revelation of His glory. And we know, for God has never failed yet, that His promise will be fulfilled.

How is it to be fulfilled for us in our time? Ultimately, this verse looks forward to the day when Jesus will return in full glory, and, as Philippians 2:10-11 confirms, the whole world shall see His glory together. Every knee shall bow, and every tongue shall confess Jesus as Lord, to the glory of God the Father. We know this will occur, for the mouth of the LORD has spoken.

The last phrase of verse 5 is a tremendous climax to the message the voice declares, for everything is sealed by the fact that the message originates with God. Can there be any doubt? If God has declared something, so it will come to pass. *The Living Bible* accentuates this surety with its paraphrase, "The Lord has spoken — it shall be." Similarly, *Today's English Version* renders, "The Lord Himself has promised this." Indeed, this verse is asserting the sovereignty of God, His majestic omnipotence, His unalterable ability to fulfill that which He declares.

This leads to some implications of this verse for each of us

today. The mouth of Yahweh has also spoken His promises of the revelation of His glory to us as individuals. The apostle Paul especially picks up this idea in 2 Corinthians 3:18, where he says that as we behold the glory of the Lord we shall be changed into His likeness, from one degree of glory to another. The glory of the LORD shall indeed be revealed *in our lives* in ways that will be observable.

God doesn't want His people to be nonentities or carbon copies of each other. Too few Christians understand that God wants to reveal His glory to the world uniquely through each of us. If the wildernesses of our lives could be properly prepared; if our valleys were lifted and our mountains brought low; if our unevennesses would become fertile plains; then truly the glory of the LORD would be revealed in our lives, and those around us would be able to observe it.

Now, lest any of us get discouraged and think we are failures because our lives don't reveal God's glory as they should, we must quickly be reminded that God is the One Who does the revealing. It is not by our own efforts that His glory shines through us. It is not by our own abilities that we can be the particular people God created us to be. In and of ourselves, we are incapable of revealing His glory. Too often we strive instead to reveal our own and discover that there is nothing there. In fact, as the apostle Paul asserts in 2 Corinthians 4:7 and 12:9, our very weaknesses, the fact that we are but clay vessels, best reveal God's glory, for they make it obvious that the transcendent power belongs to Him. This phrase from the fifth verse of Isaiah 40 again speaks to us of the mightiness of grace; the mouth of the LORD has spoken. His grace comes into our lives to transform us into the image of His Son so that His glory might be revealed in us.

This promise is made real in our lives as we heed the voice that cries out for us to prepare in the wilderness the way of the LORD. As our hearts are more and more attuned to the will of God, as we seek Him, not just to know *about* Him but also to know *Him* and abide in Him, His glory shall be revealed in us.

This verse is part of a strong scriptural theme that begins with the time of the tabernacle in the wilderness. Exodus 40 gives us the awesome picture of the filling of the tabernacle with the glorious presence of God Himself. As His glory is revealed, God pitches the tent of His presence — He "tabernacles" Himself — among the Children of Israel.

In John 1:14, this same imagery is uniquely applied when the evangelist declares, "the Word became flesh and tabernacled Himself among us." The sentence says in a very vivid way that God became human in the Person of Jesus, Who literally "pitched His tent" among men by coming to earth.

The same Greek verb, meaning "to pitch one's tent," is used in Revelation 21:3, where we read the glorious promise that the dwelling of God shall be with men, for He shall "tabernacle Himself among us." Again, the apostle Paul uses the same verb in 2 Corinthians 12:9 when he asserts that he glories in his weaknesses, for in them he experiences the "tabernacling" of God. It is in His tabernacling in our lives, especially in our weaknesses, that the glory of the LORD is revealed.

How, then, can we presume to think that the revelation is by our own efforts or abilities? The key to the whole matter of the revelation of the glory of the LORD lies in our weaknesses. When we repentantly acknowledge our failures and our presumptions, God's power *on* us can be brought to its finish. Then His glory can be revealed *through* us, and all flesh shall see it. The mouth of Yahweh has spoken, and He will do it. The LORD wants to work that kind of transformation in our lives. Are we ready to receive it?

All of this has tremendous implications for the church as a whole. Part of the reason for the church's failure to grow as it could at this time in history is that its people are not revealing the glory of the LORD. Far too easily we get caught up in a Sunday morning syndrome in which we think that our relationship to the LORD is confined to hours of worship and minutes of pious prayer, and we forget that the LORD wants to come mightily into every moment of our lives. As the way of the LORD is prepared for Him, His glory can be majestically revealed in such a way that all flesh shall see it.

The challenge before us as Christians is not what we do for the LORD, but who we are. He wants to conform us to His image, to bring us down and lift us up, to smooth us out and remove the obstructions, so that His glory can be revealed in us and through us, from one degree to another.

QUESTIONS FOR FURTHER MEDITATION:

1. In what ways is the glory of the LORD revealed to me?
2. What other places in the Scriptures speak about the LORD's glory being revealed?
3. How can I be an instrument for revealing His glory to others?
4. How can I encourage others to look for His revealing of Himself?
5. Where else in the Scriptures is it declared that God will accomplish that which He has asserted?
6. How does the fact that God's glory will soon be finally revealed in the return of Jesus Christ affect my day-to-day existence?
7. What are the implications of this verse for my church — in its large denomination and as an individual assembly of believers?

The Cry of *Sehnsucht* 6

"A voice says, 'Cry!'
And I said, 'What shall I cry?'
All flesh is grass,
and all its beauty is like the flower of the field."
Isaiah 40:6

I thought my apartment upkeep days were over. I moved into a brand new house when I first came to Olympia, and I thought that at last I was free for a few years from the bother of old things wearing out. But I had falsely assumed that everyone built things as durably as does my grandfather. I supposed that everyone strives after excellence. How disappointing to discover that things are no longer made to last! I've been shocked at poorly constructed cabinets and dismayed that the stud nails are showing through the white paint. The exterior of the house needs to be repainted, and I've only lived here three years. What has happened to the former values of quality and permanence? Perhaps you can identify with my frustration.

Yet even as I write these paragraphs I think, *Why, I'm becoming a middle-aged crank*, and I realize that my birthday is approaching much too quickly. I've always hated the merciless onrush of time. Even as a child, I hated how fast time sped by, time that I wanted to use for reading and swimming, for playing baseball and singing. Time passes away as fast as the roses. Life grows and goes as quickly as the grass.

Exactly! "All flesh is grass, and all its beauty is like the flower of the field." Our human recognition of the transience of life is just an echo of the declaration of that fact by an eternal God. The awesome question is what to do about it.

Once again in verse 6 the prophet hears the voice. This time the voice calls to him that he should cry out, that there is a message he should proclaim. When he responds, "What is it that I should proclaim?" he is told to announce the evanescence, the transience, of man. The Children of Israel experienced that impermanence when their pride and glory were shattered as they were taken into the Babylonian captivity and their temple was destroyed. They discovered that their power was fugitive; their place among the nations short-lived. This message from the prophet applied painfully to that particular moment in their history.

So it also applies particularly to our history. Today, in an age in which things are built to last only a few years in order to stimulate the economy — an age of planned obsolescence — we are distressingly aware of the impermanence of man-made things. As we behold the rapid replacements of political parties and the tragedies that befall world leaders when they are thrust from power, we become more aware of the impermanence of man. But how often do we face the fact that this message also applies to us as individuals? YOUR flesh is grass; MY beauty is like the flower of the field.

There is no word of comparison (such as *like* or *as*) in the first phrase of the message we are to proclaim. Our flesh IS grass. Just as God IS love, our flesh IS grass. Our loveliness, furthermore, is like that of a field flower — fading quickly, perhaps without ever being noticed. The Hebrew word translated "beauty" is *chesed*, more often rendered "loving kindness" or "goodness." This Hebrew word is used in all the descriptions of God's mercy, which is steadfast, unchangeable, fresh every morning in its faithfulness. While His goodness is sure and true, to be counted upon, ours is as the flowers of the field, quickly passing away. Even our attempts to be good are short-lived and unstable. So the voice says to Isaiah and to us that we should proclaim this message through the words we bring as prophets: we are to remind our society, our culture, and ourselves that nothing lasts.

Too often in our personal lives we forget this truth and mindlessly invest all our time, all our energies, all our resources, and all our care in things that will only pass away. We spend our time gaining wealth; we spend our care building power; we spend our talents achieving fame — only to discover in the end that these things, too, shall pass.

C. S. Lewis, in his insightful theory of *Sehnsucht* (discussed in his autobiography, *Surprised by Joy*, and elsewhere), made clear for me the nature of man's longing, or intense yearning. He used the German term *Sehnsucht* to describe that desire for fulfillment that nothing can satisfy. He recognized that *Sehnsucht* results from man's being made in the image of God, and he asserted that every person has it. As I've discussed that idea with both Christians and non-Christians, they have all admitted that such a longing does indeed exist in their hearts and spirits.

Lewis proposed that there are three ways that this *Sehnsucht* is handled. The first is the "fool's way." The fool thinks that if he can reach a particular goal, he will be satisfied. Consequently, he struggles and strives to achieve that goal, in the end only to discover, having reached the goal, that it cannot satisfy him.

The second way to handle *Sehnsucht* is the "sensible man's way." This wise person recognizes that the longing cannot be stilled, so he tries instead to push it under. This, too, is not successful, however, for the longing keeps surfacing, and the attempts to push it under — by means of alcohol, drugs, sex, partying, or even religious piety — must continually be redoubled to keep the lid on the growing tension and anxiety.

The third way to deal with *Sehnsucht*, Lewis suggests, is the Christian way. The believer recognizes that if he has this intense longing and (1) nothing in the world satisfies it, and (2) nothing in the world can push it under, then (3) we must be made for another world.

The reason the fool's way cannot work is found in these words from Isaiah 40:6: "All flesh is grass, and all its beauty like the flower of the field." Nothing in this world will ever satisfy our deepest longings, because everything in this world is merely temporary. We look around at all the things on which we stake our happiness and discover that they all pass away.

It is very frustrating to me that even in the happiest moments, the happiness is marred by the realization that the situation that creates it is only temporary. Every vacation with relatives from far away is affected by the terrible awareness that our time together is too short. All earthly things that produce happiness will, at some point, pass away.

This is the message we have to cry. It is a message sorely needed in our times, when the "fool's way" of striving after fulfillment is so dominant. But it seems to be such a message of despair. How can we handle such a burdensome message, this realization that all flesh is grass? Two verses later we will find the most important answer to that problem, but meanwhile we can consider from C. S. Lewis's perspective a simple fact that will enable us to cope with the burden of this message.

To face this realization that our flesh is grass does not necessarily have to lead us to despair. It will do so only if we are dependent upon our own flesh for fulfillment. It will only lead to despair if we don't have our priorities straight. The great message of the Christian faith is that we are not dependent upon these ephemeral things. The third way to handle our *Sehnsucht* is profoundly true; we are indeed made for another world!

The good news of Jesus Christ is that He has overcome the world of grass and field flowers. In fact, He uses those same elements to illustrate the basis for our hope. In Matthew 6:28 Jesus says, "Consider the lilies of the field," and then He tells us to look at their beauty and glory. Even Solomon in all his glory was not arrayed as they are, and yet, He says, they pass away. If our Father invested such care in clothing them with beauty, however, certainly we can trust Him to take care of us also.

The fact that our flesh is fleeting should do this one thing: it should drive us to total dependence upon the One Who does not pass away. That is the conclusion Lewis reached with such a stroke of genius. If the things of the world do not satisfy, if they do not push under our longings, we can come to the realization that we are indeed made for another world.

QUESTIONS FOR FURTHER MEDITATION:

1. How does my world try to hide the fact that it is temporary?
2. How do I hide that fact from myself?
3. What are some of the goals I have set for myself, thinking that if I achieved them I would be satisfied?
4. What means do I use to try to push under my discontentment?
5. What has happened as I have used these means to try to still the *Sehnsucht* deep within me?
6. How have I experienced the satisfaction of realizing that I am made for another world?
7. How might the church be crying out to the world this message that Isaiah was urged to proclaim?

The Cry of Transience 7

"The grass withers, the flower fades
when the breath of the LORD blows upon it;
surely the people is grass."

Isaiah 40:7

The editor of the campus newspaper sat in my office and told me why he chose to be a "militant atheist." "Why is there so much evil in the world if your God hasn't sent it?" My arguments were not successful in convincing him that God is not the creator of destruction.

"God is cruel, and I just cannot believe in a God who willfully hurts people." Probably you have also heard that argument from those who decry our belief in the God of the Scriptures. This seventh verse from Isaiah 40 seems at first glance to add ammunition to their attacks, for it appears to suggest that flesh withers and loveliness fades *because* the LORD sends His destructive breath upon them. How are we Christians going to answer that objection?

The argument against God seems to be fortified even more by a look at the original Hebrew of this verse. The grass dries up: the same verb root is found in Genesis 1:10, when the dry land appears on the earth by God's command. The flower fades: the noun form of this verb signifies a corpse. Both of these symptoms occur when the breath, or spirit, of Yahweh passes over them. It is troubling to find God seemingly so destructive.

The key lies, however, in the fact that these events are indeed *symptoms*. Fading happens when the LORD's breath passes over the flowers because of their nature that existed *prior* to His coming. The withering is symptomatic of the fact that flesh is grass in the first place, as the end of this verse reaffirms. "Surely" — the poetic device says, "Yes, indeed!" — "the people IS the grass."

The pronouncement, therefore, concerns the fact of God's righteousness as opposed to the weakness of man. The picture is not the image of man lying there as grass, totally the victim when God arbitrarily blows over him, and suddenly he is gone. Rather, the verse presents an honest realization of what man deserves.

This very difficult concept was clarified for me by a movie called *The Antkeeper*, which we have used in several of our youth retreats. In this film, God is represented by the gardener, and man is pictured as the flying ant. In one scene near the movie's beginning, two ants fly to a section of the garden to which the gardener has forbidden them to go. Of course, we understand this to be an analogy of the Fall. Having flown to that forbidden section, they alight on an insect-devouring plant, which immediately closes, trapping them inside. As the two ants struggle to be free, their buzzing is heard by the gardener, who stands, conversing with his son, far off on the other side of the hilltop.

With steadiness and deep anger, he slowly walks to the plant. Throughout his walk the cameras give panoramic views of the garden, all the lovely places to which the ants freely could have gone, and then return to the gardener's face to emphasize his righteous indignation. He had warned those ants for their own good. When he arrives at the closed plant with the ants buzzing inside, he grasps it firmly in his hand for just a moment.

Although I have seen the movie several times, for that moment, which seems excruciatingly long, I have been terrified. For a split second, an eternity, it seems that the gardener will crush the plant in his stern grasp. As he holds it in his hand, I know with a shudder that to be crushed is what the ants deserve. It always seems to me in that terrible moment that the gardener *should* express his righteousness by destroying those ants.

But he does not crush them. Instead, he opens the plant very carefully and draws the ants out into his hand. Eventually, his own son becomes an ant and enters their valley to save them from their destruction of themselves.

Although this small moment is not one of the major scenes in the movie, it has continued to stand out in my mind most vividly. Each time, at that point, I have understood more clearly the scriptural tension of fear and love in our relationship with God.

As New Testament Christians, we have lost sight of that tension, although it is often described in the Scriptures. For example, many of the Psalms speak both of the terror with which the poets have observed God's action in nature and of the love with which they adore their covenant God. Similarly, the apostle Paul agonizes over his bondage to sin (Rom. 7) just before exulting over the truth that nothing can separate us from the love of God (Rom. 8).

It is not possible for us truly to know the love of God unless we first have known His righteous wrath. Otherwise, we assume that it is easy for God to forgive us. We might even think it could be possible for us to earn His favor. We make grace cheap. When we totally confront our absolute hopelessness and complete depravity, however, we recognize with awe the majesty and infinity and incomprehensibility of God's love for us. God could at any moment destroy us; that is what we deserve. But He does not; that is His grace.

"The grass withers and the flower fades when the breath of the LORD blows upon it." Readers of this verse in Isaiah's time might have heard in "the breath of the LORD" a reference to the wind that comes off the Arabian desert. This wind, called a sirocco, is familiar to residents around Jerusalem. They knew, and still know, how in just a few short moments the lush spring grasses of southern Palestine are quickly destroyed when it blows. That is the inherent power of God made visible in an earthly analogy. What hope it can give us to realize that God does not arbitrarily vent His power on people. His wind does not blow by chance, for His love (chesed; see chap. 6), in contrast to ours, is faithful. He comes to us with grace.

Because we realize His awesome power, however, our love for our gracious Father in heaven is deepened. Because we know we deserve to be crushed, like the flying ants trapped in the plant, our adoration and thanksgiving are so much greater. Our purpose and meaning are so much deeper. Jesus speaks of this fact when the Pharisees criticize the woman who had anointed Him. How much more thankful she is, He asserts, because she knows how precious it is to be forgiven!

Verse 7 concludes, "Surely the people is grass." Surely we

deserve the wrath of God. *Today's English Version* translates this phrase, "People are no more enduring than grass." If we base our hopes upon our own ability to make it, we are surely going to be disappointed. We who cannot endure will inevitably fail. *The Living Bible* concludes, "and so it is with fragile man." We need to recognize that we are not able to change our fragile natures. It is not possible for us to make ourselves capable of avoiding the fate we deserve. *The Jerusalem Bible* asserts, "The grass is without doubt the people." There is no way we can miss the analogy. The voice says, "Cry," and we are told to cry out about our fate.

We need this realization that surely we are grass. In fact, we ought to remind ourselves constantly; the message is to be continually proclaimed. In one of the church's ancient prayers, used when a person has died, this phrase suggests our response to the message of verse 7: "Teach us all to number our days that we may apply our hearts unto wisdom and finally be saved." We have seen the power of God; His breath causes grass to wither and flowers to fade. We have seen the lack of power in man; surely the people is grass. These two facts together call us to number our days. Realizing who we are and who God is, we can apply our hearts unto wisdom and not trust ourselves for salvation.

QUESTIONS FOR FURTHER MEDITATION:

1. How might I become more conscious of my transience?

2. Luther spoke about dire despair as a prerequisite for knowing the love of God. What have been some times in my life when recognizing His wrath has deepened my awareness of His love?

3. What special sections of the Scriptures teach me about this tension of fear and love?

4. What are the results of an overemphasis on one side or the other in the tension of fear and love?

5. At what stages in the history of the church has one side or the other been overemphasized, and what were the results?

6. How can I keep both sides in their proper perspective and balance?

7. How might my understanding of this verse be a tool for presenting the gospel to nonbelievers?

The Cry of Absolutivity 8

"The grass withers, the flower fades;
but the word of our God will stand for ever."
Isaiah 40:8

I never liked the song until the ending. Its discordant notes were too jarring; they made me feel uncomfortable. Although its message was important, I did not like to sing the song because I found it unmelodious.

Suddenly, however, at its conclusion, my attitude changed. The chords the choir sang melted into a lovely resolution on the final words of the Scripture text, and the beauty of the sound gave me a sense of peace.

The eighth verse of Isaiah 40 presents an equally dramatic resolution. After two verses of negative assertions about withering and fading, verse 8 moves beyond those statements to the hope of something positive. There is something enduring, something to cling to. The Word of our God stands forever. It alone will not slip away in time.

An understanding of Hebrew poetic forms helps us to see the tremendous drama of this verse. The basic element in Old Testament poetry is the set of two "synonymous" parallel lines in which both phrases state essentially the same thing. This parallelism is sometimes extended by the addition of an extra phrase to the second line so that the couplet becomes "climactic," or stairlike. The parallelism is at other times inverted, or made "antithetical," in which case the second line says the opposite of the first.

In verses 6 to 8 of Isaiah 40, the prophet constructs a tremendous sequence of exquisite poetry, building to an overwhelming conclusion with a sudden antithesis. The first phrase, "All flesh is grass," is paralleled by "its beauty is like the flower of the field."

47

We might represent these lines by a^1 and a^2. Next, "the grass withers" is paralleled by "the flower fades." These could be represented by b^1 and b^2. Then, the second line (b^2) is expanded with "when the breath of the LORD blows upon it," which we might call c. Then b^1 and b^2c are followed by a return to a^1 when, for emphasis, we read, "Surely the people is grass." Finally, in verse 8 we have again our b^1 and b^2 in "The grass withers, the flower fades," and then suddenly, dramatically, these are opposed by NOT B: "The word of our God stands forever."

Suddenly across our vision sweeps the opposite of all the voice has been saying, and we are overwhelmed! This breathtaking statement is as startling as a shocking pink rose painted in the midst of a dreary scene of dull browns and rainy grays, or as a trumpet fanfare in the midst of hushed flutes and soft strings. The progression looks like this:

$$a^1 \qquad a^2$$
$$b^1 \qquad b^2c$$
$$a^1$$
$$b^1 \qquad b^2$$
NOT B!

Immediately we want to know more deeply the meaning of this NOT B. The Word of our God is not fading or withering. Greatly to the contrary, it shall indeed stand forever!

What does this brilliant shaft of light mean? How does the Word of God stand forever? Throughout the Scriptures, the concept of *Word* is pervasive. In the Old Testament, it is by the Word of His mouth that God creates. In the New Testament, it is the Word Himself, Jesus the Christ, Who becomes incarnated to "tabernacle" among us (John 1:14). The Word of God will stand forever; as He has declared it, so everything shall be accomplished (see the comments on "says your God" in chap. 1). That means nothing can change His Word, violate it, destroy it, or render it ineffective. Jesus Christ fulfilled all of God's prophetic words about Him, because He was that very Word made flesh. And now He continues to fulfill God's Word to us as He takes up residence in our lives.

There are so many implications from this verse that I hardly know where to begin. I want to run in all directions with a montage of ideas and say, "Look at this" and "Notice that" all at once.

First, and probably most important, we must recognize the stability and security that the steadfastness of God's Word provides. "When every earthly prop gives way," the old hymn asserts, "He then is all my Hope and Stay. On Christ the solid Rock I stand; all other ground is sinking sand." God's Word to us is a message of grace, and the promise of forgiveness and healing stands forever, in spite of our failures and sin. God's Word to us is love, even though we are unlovable or unloved by the world. God's Word to us is Joy in the midst of sorrow, Peace in the midst of tension, Hope in the face of anxiety. This is the basis of our faith: the realization that God's Word of salvation is true and eternal. What more can we say to describe the ecstasy His Word creates?

Second, this assertion has powerful implications for the way we minister to other people. Why give them fading fantasies or withering words when instead we could communicate to them the sure promises of God's eternal Word? This was emphasized in chapter 1 when we considered the possibility of deep and meaningful comfort in the face of tragedy. Why do we try to comfort others out of our own resources when we have all the promises of heaven at our fingertips?

Human words are folly. When we offer them to comfort, we fail to recognize that all flesh is grass. Not only are they empty gifts, but also, by wasting our time giving them, we deprive others of the rich blessings that eternal words could bestow. God's Word carries inherently within it the power to accomplish what it describes. Therefore, when I say to someone, "Grace and peace to you," those words carry within them the actual fact of grace and peace, really to be received by my listener.

Why does God's Word prove to be genuine, meaningful, substantive, and eternal? It is all these things and more because it is Truth and because His Word conveys His presence. He is there, incarnated in His Word to bring it about. The Word is made flesh to "tabernacle" among us, a concept absolutely too glorious to describe in human words.

The tremendous applicability of these words to our mixed-up times makes me want zealously to follow the instruction of the voice that says, "Cry!" People are longing for words of Truth. Our society craves substance. How powerfully this message could affect our world if we would be better at showing the world its own falliblity in light of the eternal immutability of the Word of God!

In the book *My Name Is Asher Lev*, a famous painter defines one's art by "whether or not there is a scream in him wanting to get out in a special way." His friend then immediately adds, "Or a laugh." As I pondered that bit of dialogue, I suddenly realized with dismay and with delight that Christians have both. God's people know the scream, for it is painful to acknowledge that all flesh is grass. We scream with agony as we experience the fading of the flowers.

But Christians also can't help but laugh. We laugh with victory. We laugh eternally. We bubble with Joy because God's abiding Word declares that we are His children. The promise stands forever that His grace has set us free. His eternal Word assures us of eternal life with Him.

The realization that it is a privilege to speak about this double-sided message, the artist's scream and laugh, gave rise to the whole concept for this book. It became exceedingly precious to be a part of the response to that voice which says, "Cry!" But there are more applications than just this meditation. You and I must each take these applications away from our devotional time into our worlds today. How will the Word of God go with us into our daily situations?

What promise and hope this verse gives us no matter what happens. When things go wrong, we can remember God's steadfast Word of grace. When the world's comfort is shallow and without substance, we can find, in spite of our frustrations, abiding messages of hope. When loved ones die, we know and remember the scream that all flesh is grass, but we can also rejoice in the laugh of the Word of God speaking about resurrection. When friends of the world turn away and fail us, the scream of loneliness is contradicted by the laugh of Jesus, Whose Word, "Lo, I am with you always," stands forever.

In every situation of life we confront grass and fading flowers. This eighth verse promises, however, that we can also find this laugh: the Word of the LORD abides forever! Then we can pass that laugh on to others who need to hear an abiding Word.

QUESTIONS FOR FURTHER MEDITATION:

1. How else could I describe the glorious contradiction between the ephemeral things of the world and the eternal steadfastness of God's Word?

2. What were some times when I ministered to people with only superficial comfort?

3. How could I have given them an eternal and abiding Word instead?

4. What are some of the situations my life has entailed in the last few days, and what were the screams in them?

5. What were the laughs?

6. What goals could I set for myself in order to get to know the eternal Word of God better?

7. What are some of the implications of this verse for my church and its ministries?

The Cry for Heralding 9

"Get you up to a high mountain,
O Zion, herald of good tidings;
lift up your voice with strength,
O Jerusalem, herald of good tidings,
lift it up, fear not;
say to the cities of Judah,
'Behold your God!'"

Isaiah 40:9

"I want to shout it from the mountaintops," a girl exclaims to her best friend as she announces her engagement. "And if you can't hear us, we'll yell a little louder," the fans scream as they parade through their hometown streets after winning the league basketball championship. What do love stories and sports pride have to do with Isaiah 40:9? Simply, they illustrate the principles of heralding good news. "Get up to a high mountain," Zion is told. "Lift up your voice with strength," Jerusalem is commanded. If you have good news to tell, make sure you are visible to all, and then say it again louder, just to be sure it's heard!

I love the poetic repetition of this verse, with its thrilling emphasis on the privilege that is ours. We could modernize the prophet's reiteration in this way: "Shout it from the mountaintops, you who are messengers of the good news. Yell a little louder, you who are messengers of the good news. Yell still more; don't be afraid. Say to each and every one who dwells in your land, 'Look! Your God is here!'"

Isaiah's words to Zion can be applied immediately to us. We are the people of God in our time, and the need for the message that God is here is even more critical in our New Testament age. This is the kind of pep-rally encouragement we all need to stir us up. We tend to sit and ponder and get all afraid, and fail to realize the nature of the good news we have to proclaim. Look at this message we are to cry out: our God is here! How can we be so unmoved by such good news?

How are we to cry it? The commands of this verse follow a deliberate progression. First we are told to declare the good news, not from the valleys or in the churches, but boldly from the top of the mountains, out in the open. Both words from verse 4 are put together here to emphasize the high places of the mountaintops. We are to get ourselves up to those lofty peaks as pilgrims go up to the temple (see Psalms 113-118, which are the "Songs of the Ascents"). Once there, we are to fulfill our function as messengers of very important good news. The idea of heralding is an intensive participle; we are to proclaim it exuberantly. We are to shout it down so that all can hear.

Next, we are to exalt, or lift up, our voices with great strength. The word *strength* here anticipates its climactic use in verse 31, wherein those who wait upon the LORD find it renewed. This phrase seems to accentuate the extra effort; once we have gotten ourselves up, we are to extend our voices even more to make sure the message is heard. This extra effort is again called for by the poetic repetition of the verb, "lift it up."

But wait. Perhaps the factor holding us back is our fear. The positive encouragement is suddenly interrupted, almost as if to say, "What's the matter? Is fear the problem? Then cast it aside!". Immediately, then, this negative reprimand is swallowed up by the glorious content of our heralding, "Behold your God!" We are to introduce Him to the cities of Judah.

This geographical designation, spoken as it was to Zion, seems to connote her neighbors, as if she were told, "Say to those who live around you." What an evangelism program! We have the privilege of saying to our friends next door and down the block, "Our God has arrived!"

Churches try so frantically to institute evangelism programs, and therein lies their problem. I'm not opposed to evangelism programs *per se.* Many of them are very well prepared; I find them very helpful for teaching people how to give witness of their faith. The problem with them arises, however, because too easily they can cause us to lose sight of the fact that our evangelism cannot be programmed. Our witness comes from a spontaneous reaction to the Joy-full realization that our God is here.

When was the last time you were greatly excited about something? Was it hard for you to tell someone else about it? Did you sit on your hands and get all nervous and stew and fret about whether you'd have the right words? Why is it that we can speak so easily about the good things that happen in our lives? The previous three verses reminded us that these very good things are only going to pass away. Now here we have this message that abides forever — our God is here! — and yet we are actually afraid to tell other people.

One of the greatest needs in our Christian churches is to recover the significance of this verse for our times. We need the boldness of Isaiah, the exuberance of the early Christians, the contagion of those people who cannot help but tell those around them that God is here. Getting up to a high mountain symbolizes getting to where we can be seen. I don't think that means we are to be ostentatious or flamboyant about our witness. I don't think it means we have to stand on a soapbox on the street corner. In fact, the contemporary evangelical bandwagon has recently been criticized for adopting "show biz" techniques that give the Gospel the ill-suited flavor of the hard-sell approach.

On the contrary, I think it does mean that we can't just keep quiet or merely mumble under our breath. It does mean that in our Joy over the presence of the LORD we can freely witness openly, even if it might mean that we become a target for persecution. The nature of the good news is that we don't mind being seen; we find it a privilege to tell the good news about the One we see, especially because those down in the valley need to hear that God is here.

In the Hebrew culture of Isaiah's time, when the bearer of good tidings, such as victory in battle, got up to a high mountain to shout, he didn't have to worry about how he would be received. He knew that everybody was waiting for the message he had to give. Too often we fail to realize the goodness of our message and, consequently, we get embarrassed or ashamed about it. We don't have to be ashamed, Paul asserts (Rom. 1:16). Accordingly, our being able to shout loud enough is a natural outflow of our being overwhelmed by how good the message is. We don't have to be afraid to proclaim it; after all, those who would persecute us are only grass. The Word we proclaim will bear itself out as Truth, for it endures forever. Our task is simply to introduce those who listen to the fact that God is here.

Besides its applicaton to our evangelism, this verse carries important implications for ministry among the members of the Body of Christ. According to verse 9, we are commanded to lift our voices, to fear not, and to say to the cities of Judah, "Behold your

God." Often we might be up on mountains when other members of the Body are down in valleys. When they have trouble seeing that God is here, we can minister from a different perspective and point out the good news to them. Herein lies the secret of building up one another. It is our privilege to take others by the hand and get up to the high mountains to shout, "God is here." This is the center of the gospel. Without God we have nothing. If He is here, behold — we have everything.

One final observation: What gives this verse its tremendous freedom is that we are called by the name, "heralds of good tidings." The person who serves as a herald is totally responsible to the source of his message. He does not have to worry about the reaction to his words; that isn't his responsibility. His only responsiblity is to proclaim as faithfully as he can the message he has been given.

We are called to be heralds. (That is why I like so much the name of my publisher.) We do not have to fear how our words of encouragement or our words of witness will be received. We are called only to report faithfully these good tidings that are ours to give: "Behold your God!" All we must do is tell others that God is here; the rest is up to Him.

QUESTIONS FOR FURTHER MEDITATION:

1. What people that I know specifically need to hear that God is here?

2. How can I gently and reverently (see 1 Pet. 3:15) communicate to those people that God is here?

3. What kinds of fears keep me from telling others that God is here?

4. How can I become more aware of the fullness of His presence?

5. What are the strong points of my church's evangelism program (if it has one) or its witness to the neighbors?

6. What are the weaknesses of my church's witness, and what can I do about them?

7. How can I safeguard my own witness and that of my church from phoniness and superficiality?

The Cry of Might 10

*"Behold, the Lord GOD comes with might,
and his arm rules for him;
behold, his reward is with him,
and his recompense before Him."*

Isaiah 40:10

The winning boxer raised his arm triumphantly and gave a great shout of joy. His victory pose was splashed across all the front pages of the newspapers' sports sections. There could be no doubt that he had been the strongest. He even took his best friends out for a victory celebration.

Just like a newspaper description, Isaiah 40:10 invites us to behold the victory pose of the Lord GOD. He will come with might, and His arm will rule for Him. He will bring along a victory celebration. The previous verse had announced with Joy that indeed He does come, but now we see how He comes. Each phrase adds a significant dimension to the total picture.

First, it is the Lord GOD Who comes with might. The Hebrew words are *Adonai Yahweh*, divine ruler and covenant God. He comes with all the fullness of His divinity and sovereignty, but also as Yahweh, the great "I AM." His might is directed toward the fulfilling of His covenant promises, the perfecting of His relationship with His people. Consequently, we see a fulfillment of this phrase when God came to deliver His people out of the Babylonian captivity. He was faithful to His promise to restore the remnant. The coming of Jesus was another fulfillment of this verse, and we look forward to His coming again, when all His glorious might will fully be made known. Finally, we need to remember that He comes as Adonai Yahweh to us today, a God of might, channeled to fulfill His promises to us.

How frightful it would be if God exerted His might without the covenant relationship! How terrible God would appear to us if we

57

did not know that His power will have dominion for our benefit!
His arm upraised to rule for Him would terrify us if we did not
know the graciousness of His covenant love.

The Living Bible translates these first two phrases, "Yes, the
Lord God is coming with mighty power; he will rule with awesome strength." We think back to previous verses that spoke
about the emptiness of man and the ephemerality of his life, and
in strong contrast to that we see here the fullness of God's power.
The majesty and infinity of His might will be illustrated much
more thoroughly later in this fortieth chapter of Isaiah, but these
first two phrases in verse 10 offer a brief introduction to the
concept.

The second set of parallel phrases presents the picture of the
gifts the Lord GOD brings with Him. The nature of the reward
that is with Him is not specified. The Hebrew word means
"wages," coming from the root meaning "to hire." The term implies
the fulfillment of God's promises to those who serve Him. He has
promised to His people rewards of rest, security, and victory.
How different this is from the pattern of the world's rewards,
which pass away and force us to settle for less than the best.
When our covenant God comes in His power, He will bring us the
best. As James reminds us, "Every good endowment and every
perfect gift is from above, coming down from the Father of lights
with whom there is no variation or shadow due to change" (1:17).

The word translated "recompense" carries us in the opposite
direction, into the past. The term refers to works that God has
already accomplished. These will go before His face in the victory
celebration. The meaning of this picture is not entirely clear.
Perhaps the implication is that everyone who observes will recognize that God has accomplished all the deeds that are made
known. Maybe in the midst of the experience of victory, we will
realize how God has prepared the way beforehand so that such a
moment might take place. Perhaps one of the most important
implications for our time is the reminder that we do nothing by
our own power or grace, but are only doing the "good works,
which God prepared beforehand, that we should walk in them"
(Eph. 2:10).

Combining the two sets of figures used in this verse, we might imagine kings returning from battle with the spoils of victory. If that is the intent of the picture, we might specifically recognize that the Lord GOD comes having defeated Satan and rescued from his grasp all whom he had enslaved within his powers. In that case, the victory procession might include us. When the Lord GOD comes with His reward with Him, He brings the redeemed ones, the ones saved from slavery, the ones brought back from forces that might control us. That is the implication of the *Today's English Version* translation, which says, "The sovereign Lord is coming to rule with power, bringing with him the people he has rescued."

One of the great implications of this verse for us is the strong hope that it gives to carry us through difficult situations. We can trust that our covenant God goes with us, and we know that He comes with might on our behalf. We can enter boldly into any kind of situation we might face. We do not have to trust our own power to be able to handle difficulty, for it is the arm of the LORD that rules for Him. He has raised His arm on our behalf.

Another picture this verse creates is the theme of the Lord GOD laden with gifts. He does not come empty-handed. Many people fear becoming Christians because they think they will have to give everything up. It's the old false notion that Christians never have any fun. Imagine the kinds of surprises the LORD carries with Him as His rewards!

I am sure each of us has experienced at times the pleasant surprise when suddenly the arm of the LORD has been raised for us or we have seen a reward from Him being carried with Him as He comes to us. I experienced that kind of surprise last Friday. I had gone to church for a normal work day, but I suddenly discovered that, since my Hebrew professor would be unavailable to meet with me on Monday, it was necessary for me to travel to Portland immediately to study with him for the background of this manuscript. I was a little anxious about all the driving (five hours altogether) because I had stayed up late the night before to study.

Just when I was getting ready to leave my office, a close friend stopped by just to say, "Hi." Because he had not been by for a long time, it was a special treat to see him. Even better, however, was his offer to drive me to Portland. What a coincidence that this day of all days he should come for a visit, and what a special gift his offer of transportation was! Not only did I not have to fight fatigue in driving alone, but our conversation was spiritually encouraging for both of us, as well. My work with the professor was exciting and rewarding; the scenery of the summer day was especially beautiful. My appreciation for everything all day was heightened by the special awareness of God's gifts that the particularly surprising gift of a precious friendship had awakened.

A simple illustration perhaps, but when we have such experiences we understand more deeply the point of this verse. Already we see God using His power on our behalf and bringing His gifts as He comes to us. Some day we will be able to see all His power, and the gifts He brings to us on that day will be eternal.

QUESTIONS FOR FURTHER MEDITATION:

1. What are some of the names for God that especially signify His covenant relationship with His people?

2. How has the Lord GOD come to me with might?

3. How have I seen the arm of the LORD raised on my behalf?

4. What rewards has He brought with Him to bless my life?

5. In times of my service for Him, how have I felt rewarded?

6. What are some ways in which God's prior deeds have been readily apparent to me as I have experienced victories in my life?

7. How can I prepare for Christ's coming again with all His power and rewards? (Please be careful with this question, lest we begin to think or act with the subconscious thought that we can earn His rewards.)

The Cry of Gentleness 11

"He will feed his flock like a shepherd,
he will gather the lambs in his arms,
he will carry them in his bosom,
and gently lead those that are with young."
Isaiah 40:11

Where is God when you need Him? Tonight I chose to rewrite the beginning of this chapter because I need the gentleness of the LORD's shepherding. I need to think about His promise to care for us tenderly.

All evening my heart has been wrapped in a fog of despair. I feel I have never been treated so cruelly as I was tonight by a person very special to me. I begged that person to accept my love, but my pleas to restore our relationship were rejected with a stony aloofness. My needs for a reconciling touch were shrugged away. Sobbing to the walls, I stumbled to another room and cried out through the window to the sky.

After my tears subsided, I opened my Bible to Isaiah 40 to read some words of comfort. "Like a shepherd," verse 11 begins in the Hebrew. I don't think that I have ever known such pain as I experienced tonight, but God's Word offers a tremendous comfort in this declaration that our LORD comes to His own like a shepherd. Can there really be such a comfort? For me? Tonight? Yes, for it is the Lord GOD Who comes like a shepherd!

What a gently loving contrast this verse forms with the preceding one! The same Hebrew word for arm occurs in both, but the arm that ruled and declared God's might in verse 10 is now used gently to gather the lambs whom He shepherds. This is a picture to be cherished. We need to know that God exerts His power and strength on our behalf. But we also need to know that in His dealings with us, He comes like a shepherd. Through His Word the Shepherd came gently to comfort me tonight.

"Like a shepherd His flock He feeds." The nurturing that takes place in our relationship with the LORD is doubly emphasized in the Hebrew because the word for "shepherd" comes from the verb root meaning "to feed," and, thus, the root both begins and ends the phrase. The LORD does not leave us without the means by which we can be strengthened. No, rather, He gently provides for our feeding in all situations. A strong hope lies in this promise that wherever we go or whatever we do, as we stay in a right relationship with the LORD, He will provide for our deepest needs. Even tonight, when there is no one here to comfort me, my needs for His gentle caring are met by the messages of comfort in His Word.

I remember once when Bob, a student of mine at the University of Idaho, worried about what would happen when he left the university and was no longer exposed to the Bible studies and fellowship available on the campus. Months after he left, however, he came back for a visit and announced that in every place to which he had gone, the Lord had provided for his spiritual needs.

Dave, another student, experienced the same thing even more dramatically. As he left for another university and graduate work, he recognized the importance of nurturing in the Word of God. Deliberately becoming involved in a quiet discipling relationship with his roommate, he found his faith immeasurably strengthened. Soon he became a leader among the Christians on that campus, and now, as I observe him in his new marriage, I am amazed at the strong man of God and Christian leader he has become.

With what gentleness the LORD makes certain that we are fed! He feeds us through the disciplines of our own quiet times and private meditations. He nurtures us by means of teachers and preachers and practicers of His Word. He sustains us through the strength of churches and assemblies of believers. He feeds us through music. He uplifts us with lovely sunsets and flowers. Truly, the LORD is our shepherd; we shall not want.

Second, verse 11 adds not only that He feeds us, but also that He gathers us up in His arms. "I am Jesus' little lamb," we sing, and it is a picture to treasure. I'm not too excited about the fact that lambs are quite dumb and that I fit that characterization. Yet when I face the reality of my life, I have to admit it is true. But there is more to the picture than just the foolishness of the lamb.

The picture I really love is the image of a strong shepherd gathering lambs into His arms to embrace them and fondle them, making sure they feel protected and secure. Don't you sometimes need to be sheltered? Whether you are male or female, young or old, I am sure that at certain times you need to feel safe.

Sometimes I feel so defenseless and vulnerable that I need to be protected from everything going on around me. Sometimes I feel so all alone that I need more than anything to be wrapped up in God's arms and securely enfolded in His love. That is the Joy to me of the name Habakkuk, which means, "God's love embrace."

But we are not embraced only individually, in isolation. Verse 11 declares that God gathers the lambs. The modern term for a collective community, the Jewish "kibbutz," comes from the verb used here. This Word of God is made real — incarnated today — in the fellowship of Christian believers. The way I experience God's love-embrace is through the care, affection, and security provided by my friends in Christ. One of the most significant dimensions of a worshiping community must be this kind of spiritual embrace.

When those who participate in the "gathering" express their relationship with a touch, God's embrace is made even more real. Too often churches fail to provide the comforting this embrace entails. This kind of security could be freely offered to all and by all who participate in each assembly of believers.

The last two phrases of verse 11 amplify the picture. The LORD lifts up the lambs to carry them in His bosom. Here the Hebrew verb we translate "to carry" is the same one that described the lifting up of the valleys in verse 4. Furthermore, the Shepherd gently leads those that are with young. When we are young and not able to walk, the LORD provides the transportation, and it is uplifting. When we are older and don't know which direction to go, He shows us the way. The verb translated "leads" implies in the Hebrew a bringing to a place of rest or a watering place. That implication reinforces again the feeding and nurturing stressed at the beginning of the verse.

These last two phrases imply a significant progression — from being a young one, carried, to being a ewe-with-young, nurtured

and guided. This is the great emphasis of Watchman Nee's book
Sit, Walk, Stand, a study in the book of Ephesians. He explains
that we are not able to walk in the Christian faith unless we have
first learned to sit. We must begin by resting in the Lord and
allowing Him to do everything on our behalf. That is the essential
understanding of grace that is the foundation of our faith.

We first must be carried by the Shepherd before we are able to
bear young ourselves. As the Shepherd gathers us into the community of believers in the beginning of our life of faith, we must
rely totally on the grace of Christ. He is the One Who carries us
and provides for all our needs. Then, as our faith grows, we grow
more able to nurture others. Although we might become the
spiritual parents for the birth of new Christians, however, we
must still rely totally on the leading of the LORD. We cannot be
mother ewes and nurture our young unless we are directly
following the Shepherd.

The implications of this message are profound. The life proclaimed in this verse begins in the need for total submission to the
action of God on our behalf. Then it invites us to devoted, inti-
mate following of His way so that we can be mothers to those who
are new in the faith. Notice that the Shepherd does not lead us
with the might of the previous verse. Instead, He leads us gently,
so we want to follow. Furthermore, His gentle leading stirs in us
the desire to pass on His gentle nurturing to those who are
spiritually in our care.

The New Jerusalem Bible translates this last phrase, "leading
to their rest the mother ewes." This must always be a fundamen-
tal understanding throughout our Christian lives: the Shepherd is
always leading us to our rest. The principle of grace underlies the
whole picture. He Who declares Himself the Good Shepherd (John
10:11, 14) also claims to be the Way (John 14:6). We cannot do
anything by our own strength. The might exerted for us in verse
10 is gently channeled in verse 11, but still it is the might of God.

We do not ever accomplish anything for God's Kingdom by our
own will-power or abilities. Always we are able to serve the LORD
and nurture His flock only by following the gentle Shepherd Who
lifts us and leads us to our rest.

QUESTIONS FOR FURTHER MEDITATION:

1. How can I receive the feeding the Shepherd wants to provide me, and why do I often run from His nurturing instead?

2. How can I more thoroughly experience the security of His love's embrace?

3. In what ways do I try to make it on my own as a little lamb, and lose the way?

4. Whom has the Shepherd committed into my care?

5. How might I make better use of His means of grace to follow Him more faithfully and nurture more effectively the young in my care?

6. What are some of the implications of this verse for churches?

7. How can this verse be helpful to me in times of depression, doubt, or fear?

The Cry of Wonder 12

*"Who has measured the waters in the hollow of his hand
and marked off the heavens with a span,
enclosed the dust of the earth in a measure
and weighed the mountains in scales
and the hills in a balance?"*

Isaiah 40:12

First, imagine all the raindrops in the world. Then add all the snowflakes and hailstones, the fog and the mists. Next, bring in all the creeks and ponds and puddles. Finally, add all the glaciers and snowpacks, the streams and rivers, the wells and underground rivers and springs, and even all the lakes and the mammoth oceans. All the waters of the earth, added all together — and God holds them in a single handful! Incredible!

Whereas in verse 11 we saw the gentleness of God, now in verse 12 we catch a glimpse of the awe-inspiring majesty of God. I love the way that the images of the Hebrew faith are so tangible. We call it anthropomorphism when human qualities and characteristics are assigned to God so that we might better understand Him. We have to use human images such as those of weighing and measuring to at least begin to comprehend the infinity of God's greatness, and yet, after all the profound pictures and the application of these minute measurements to magnificent things, we begin to realize the incomprehensibility of our subject. To suggest even that we can begin to grasp the character and extent of God's majesty is absurd.

The entire verse is set up as a rhetorical question based on the initial interrogative pronoun, "who." Of course, there is only one answer. The Lord GOD is the only one capable of such feats. Each phrase is valuable, however, for stirring up a deeper awe, for filling us with wonder at the incredible sovereignty of God.

"Who has measured the waters in the hollow of His hand?" Even if we limited our picture to just one of the bodies of water

67

mentioned at the beginning of this chapter, the image is mind-boggling. Try to imagine a person holding in the palm of his hand the Pacific Ocean. Having grown up in Ohio, far from oceans, and living now in a city close to the Pacific Ocean, I am still like a little child when I stand on the shore of that vast body of water. I am overwhelmed by its thundering waves, its myriad forms of life, its infinite variety of hues — the multifaceted splendor of the sea. To begin to think about the size is an astonishing experience. But then to go one step further and imagine the Lord GOD holding that in the palm of a single hand is too staggering!

The Hebrew form that we translate "hollow of His hand" occurs only three times in the Old Testament. In the other two places it is plural, referring to handfuls, such as in the phrase, "handfuls of barley." Only in Isaiah 40:12 is the word singular. Astounding! God needs only one hand to hold all that water. And even as we are dumbfounded by that picture, we realize how inadequate it is, for, indeed, God created all that water with just the Word of His mouth (another anthropomorphic term). Because Isaiah has suggested the picture, however, to study it even in its inadequacy gives us a bit better idea of the tremendous might and power the Lord GOD possesses.

The second picture just makes me laugh. The measure of a span is the distance between the ends of one's little finger and one's thumb when the hand is fully spread. That makes the distance of one-half a cubit. Imagine God — especially if we see Him in that ridiculous caricature of Father Time, with a long, white beard and a cane — establishing whole galaxies by the spanfull! Whole light years of space are encompassed by His fingers. I wonder how many solar systems can be hidden under His little finger nail!

The verb form of this second phrase actually means "to mete out" or "to make right according to the standard." Thus, together with the initial interrogative pronoun of the verse that is assumed here, this phrase asks, "Who regulated the heavens by the span?" The picture is so funny that it forces me to laugh at our silly stupidity. The whole point of the picture is that if God is capable of doing such a thing, aren't we foolish not to trust Him? Aren't we stupid not to realize that this power will be exercised on our behalf by our covenant God (see the meditation for v. 10)? Whereas man measures the distance between stars in light years (another measurement too incredible to imagine), God determines those same spaces with the distance between His thumb and His pinky.

The third phrase of verse 12 says literally, "and all in the third part the dust of the earth." There is no verb in this phrase, and the unit of measurement is thought by most scholars to mean the third part of an ephah, or about a quarter of a gallon. All the sands of the ocean beaches, all the dust in your house and mine, all the dirt that all kids everywhere bring home from their play — all the dust of the earth God can hold, or measure, in His quart-sized bucket.

And then, as if that weren't demonstration enough, He weighs all the mountains in a single scale and all the hills in a double balance. Now both the terms of verse 4 are used in the plural to assert that God assesses all of them critically.

The last picture is the funniest of all to me. Imagine, if you will, a single scale sitting on a table. And there is God, tossing on Mount McKinley, Mount Everest, all the Himalayas, the Alps, and the Rockies, and then assessing their worth! Living close to Mount Rainier, I am fascinated that we can drive for hours and not seem to get any closer to that majestic peak. Once while coming back from the east side of the Washington Cascades, we suddenly rounded a curve, and there, right in front of us in all its glory, towered Mount Rainier, four or five times taller than I would have expected it to be. And yet, Isaiah says, the Lord GOD can easily pick up that mountain and, with a flick of His wrist, toss it on the scale!

I'm sure that by now you are realizing with me the utter folly of human perception. We can't even begin to imagine what God is like; all our pictures are shockingly dazzling, and yet they don't even scratch the surface of the unutterable wonder of His inexpressible infinity. Why are we such blind fools in our presumptions that we do not trust this God Who exercises His might on our behalf? "Who can do these things?" Isaiah asks, and the galaxies sing out the answer. Indeed, "The heavens are telling the glory of God; and the firmament proclaims his handiwork" (Psalm 19:1). Then how shall we respond?

QUESTIONS FOR FURTHER MEDITATION:

1. What images might I use to describe the infinity of God?

2. What does this verse teach me about the character of God?

3. What does this verse teach me about myself?

4. Why are these pictures of God's inconceivable majesty not terrifying?

5. When measurements of such trivial size refer to such vast entities, how do I feel? That is, what emotions did I experience when reading this chapter?

6. How can verses such as this be used to deepen the praises of my worship?

7. What are the implications of this verse for the world?

The Cry for the Counselor 13

"Who has directed the Spirit of the LORD,
or as his counselor has instructed him?"
Isaiah 40:13

It seemed to me that my life was falling apart. Health problems had prevented my accepting a teaching position in Hong Kong. I thought, perhaps, that I should go on to graduate school, but I had not received any of the scholarships or fellowships for which I'd been a nominee. Nothing seemed to fit together. The only offer I had was to teach English while doing graduate work at the University of Idaho. But it didn't make any sense that I should go there.

"Now, God," I would often say in my prayers, "are you sure you know all the facts?" I figured that if He had them all straight, He would certainly do things my way. What folly and presumption! Who would dare to think that God needs our assistance?

Rhetorically, Isaiah asks the same question in verse 13. He asks who has directed the Spirit of the LORD or as His counselor has instructed Him. Obviously the answer is that no one can, that no one does, and yet how often we do try.

The first question in the Hebrew is made doubly ironic by the occurrence of a repeated verb. Isaiah uses the same term that he chose to describe God's regulating of the heavens in verse 12 to ask now who it is that establishes God. Can anyone have the ability to direct Him, He Who directed the ordering of the heavens with His thumb and little finger? We must learn to take seriously the majesty of God.

The word for "Spirit" bears many significant connotations in the Old Testament. It signifies the powerful agent through which God has done His creative work. The LORD's Spirit brings life and

71

makes us alive; He brought order out of chaos. Who could dare to try to order Him?

The form of the verb in the poetic parallel of the second line doubly reinforces the folly of these two questions. Who has thought that he could cause God to know his counsel? Who can stand by to instruct the One Who is Himself called by the name of Wonderful Counselor (Isa. 9:7)?

Down through the ages, Isaiah's words have mocked the folly of those who presume to instruct the Spirit of the LORD. A man's mind might plan his way, but the LORD directs his steps (Prov. 16:9). Many people after Isaiah's time must have thought for sure that they knew the best way to restore the Children of Israel from their captivity. It took men like Ezra and Nehemiah, faithful leaders who listened to instruction from Yahweh, to stir up the people to reconstruct the city of Jerusalem and its temple, to restore the nation according to God's plan.

Peter tried to instruct Jesus for the fulfilling of His office by rebuking Him when He prophesied His suffering and death (Matt. 16:22). How little Peter understood that through His Son, God was going to fulfill His purposes for the whole world and not just for the Children of Israel, to rescue them from Roman rule.

Similarly, how little we understand the purposes of God for our lives and, through us, for others. Our perspectives are severely limited. Consequently, it seems that many times when we pray, we try to instruct the LORD instead of waiting for His direction, instead of submitting to His perfect will. We pray as if to say, "LORD, I've got to straighten You around." In our presumptions, we begin to think we know better than He how our lives ought to be run. We assume that we know best what is good for us, where we should go, and how our lives should develop.

What idolatry this verse points out in our lives! We probably think this way far more often than we realize. Any time we presume to dictate to the LORD the direction things should go, we assume we know better than He all the elements that compose our existence. We have the audacity to think that we can see far more than the God Who reigns in the heavens and marks them off with the span.

We might ask, then, about the value of prayer. Why should we spend time putting into words our feelings and concerns or our needs and cares? The LORD knows them all anyway. He doesn't need our instruction. He knows perfectly well who we are, how we feel, and what we desire. Does this verse indirectly negate the value of prayer?

I think not. One of the values of prayer for me arises from this very fact that the LORD does not need anyone to counsel Him. In our words of praise, we remember His power and majesty. We are reminded of His infinite wisdom and care, and, consequently, we are assured that He is watching over everything that concerns us (1 Pet. 5:7), and that He will work all things together for our good (Rom. 8:28).

Furthermore, as we pray to Him about our perceptions of ourselves and others, we find them deepened and clarified. He has promised to give wisdom to those who ask (James 1:5-8).

In times of petition and intercession, our own desperation because of our weakness and sin is made more clear. We can come to recognize as we pray for God's action on behalf of others that He wants to use us for the fulfilling of His purposes. What better picture of grace is there than this: that no one directs the Spirit of the LORD, that no one can be His instructor, and yet He deigns to use us and to make us valuable members of His Body. In His perfection He hears our cry and comes to comfort us, to give us guidance, and to instruct us in the way we should go.

It is significant that in the New Testament the Spirit of the LORD is called the Counselor (John 14:16). Although Isaiah at the time of his writing had at best an unclear concept of the Trinity, and although this verse does not specifically refer to the Spirit as the third Person in the triune Godhead, yet Jesus reveals to us purposefully that the Spirit is sent in order for us to receive His counseling. That Spirit has been given. He has been poured out corporately upon, and indwells personally, each one of us who believe in Jesus Christ. This is the great Joy of our lives as New Testament believers — not only that we recognize that the Spirit of the LORD doesn't need directions and that no one can instruct Him, but also that He personally dwells in our hearts to direct our lives and guide us by His instruction and counsel.

Isaiah's rhetorical question forces us to admit that no one directs the Spirit or counsels Him, although we often try. Much to the contrary, instead of attempting to inform Him, we need to learn to have our lives informed by Him. Although we can't in this brief meditation outline a whole doctrine of the Spirit-filled and Spirit-led life, we can allow this verse to stir up in us a greater desire for such a lifestyle.

This problem is clearly pinpointed by Isaiah: we are not as directed by the Spirit as we could be because too often we are trying too hard to direct Him. When we are caught up in our own perceptions of how things should go, we cannot be open enough to see and hear and feel the insights, commands, and nudges the Spirit is trying to give us.

Perhaps the example from the beginning of this chapter might make this principle more clear. After I was denied health clearance to teach at the school in Hong Kong, I faced the difficult choice between teaching in a Lutheran high school or going on to graduate school. I wanted to follow the LORD's will and had prayed that if He wanted me to go to graduate school, the finances would be provided. The week before leaving for Easter vacation, I agonized over the decision because I had not received either of the national fellowships for which I'd been recommended by my college. Not until a caring professor showed me that the instructional assistantship I'd been offered at the University of Idaho could be the Lord's way of providing the finances did I realize the clarity of His direction. Almost a year later, busily involved in teaching "Literature of the Bible" at the university and leading a Bible study group for high school students, I was told by a member of that fellowship that during that very week when I had decided to come to Idaho, she and her friends had prayed that God would send them a Bible study leader.

So specific — but I had almost missed the Spirit's direction because I had already decided how the finances for graduate study should be obtained.

"Who has directed the Spirit of the LORD?" Isaiah asks. No one has. And no one can. Maybe you and I should give up trying.

QUESTIONS FOR FURTHER MEDITATION:
1. What have been some times when I have tried to direct the LORD according to my own perceptions of things?

2. When were some times in which I knew that the LORD's instructions applied most specifically to my life?

3. How do I know if I possess the Spirit? (Be careful to be scriptural here.)

4. How can I learn to listen more carefully to the Spirit?

5. How can my life become more specifically directed by Him?

6. Does God have a specific plan for my moment-by-moment life or, rather, a more general direction in which I should go, making my own decisions on the way? What scriptural evidence is there for my opinion?

7. What is the relationship of my free will to the fact that God has a plan for my life and gives direction by means of His Spirit's guidance?

The Cry of God's Understanding 14

*"Whom did he consult for his enlightenment,
and who taught him the path of justice,
and taught him knowledge,
and showed him the way of understanding?"*

Isaiah 40:14

My pleading with her was in vain. She lived across the hall in a graduate student apartment dorm. I begged her with all the love I had to reconsider her decision to move in with her boyfriend. She went anyway, but in a few weeks she was back. He had dumped her, and she had discovered with great pain that "If it feels good, do it" was not a workable philosophy for life.

"Life, liberty, and the pursuit of happiness!" "Reason, nature, happiness, progress, and liberty!" "Liberty, equality, and brotherhood!"

Throughout the history of civilization there have been sporadic times of supposed enlightenment, and men have adopted slogans such as those above to promote a particular lifestyle or philosophy of government as a means to happiness and fulfillment. Each of those periods has been characterized by a grand optimism, a conviction that man has become more reasonable and will, therefore, be able to solve all his problems. Significantly, however, each of those eras has been followed by a time when men have recognized that their reason is not able to carry them to the heights they endeavor to reach. Those periods after the euphoria are marked by a severe decline in morality or in justice — humanity destroying itself. After all the fanfare, the brazen presumptuousness of the glory of reason, comes the crushing realization that man is, despite his pretensions, not so smart.

But look, on the other hand, says the prophet, at God. Whom did He consult for His enlightenment? The very question forces us to discover that the epitome of enlightenment — in fact, the

77

only true enlightenment — comes from Him. Each time man has turned back to God in the spirit of repentance, revival, and reform, there has followed a time of great moral endeavor.

Consider, for example, these tremendously humanitarian deeds that followed the Wesleyan revival: the abolition of slavery, the securing of better labor conditions, the elimination of child labor, and many others less well known. A relationship with the One Who needs no one else to give Him understanding will result in clearer insight and deeper awareness both of the problems of society and the means for solving those problems. Man's enlightenment, on the other hand, only causes him to turn in to himself in exaltation of his own reason.

Second, in verse 14 the prophet asks us, "Who has taught the LORD the path of justice?" As we survey our world, we discover that thorough justice is nowhere to be found. At various times, men with great humanitarian motives have sought justice, but have been incapable of producing it perfectly. As long as man's nature is to seek the best for himself, he will ultimately deal unjustly with others. Recognizing that true justice is only possible in the freedom from self found in a deep relationship with the LORD causes us to hunger and thirst after His righteousness, to desire His justice to pervade our land. History shows that in times of deep spirituality, justice is more frequently attained.

"Who has taught the LORD knowledge?" *The Jerusalem Bible* translates this third phrase, "Who has discovered for him the most skillful ways?" *The Living Bible* says, "Did he need instruction as to what is right and best?"

To gain knowledge in our specialized, high-technology society is a perplexing problem. The more we learn, the more we realize how much we don't know. I am astounded at the size of vast libraries, and then aghast when I discover they still don't have the book I am seeking. The LORD doesn't need vast libraries to give Him knowledge or skill; He knows it all already. I struggle so hard in my attempts to learn Hebrew or Chinese. It's staggering to think about all the thousands of languages that God knows. He has a "doctorate" in every single field of study. He's got ALL the facts.

"Who has caused Him to discern reasons?" is the final question of this verse. The last noun in the Hebrew text is derived from the same root as the initial verb of the verse, so it ties all four phrases together with the initial "Who." The term signifies the reason, but it is used here in a plural form to indicate all understanding and insight, logic and thought. It suggests the true enlightenment; consequently, the phrase questions whether anyone can cause God to perceive the Truth of reason. As is the case with all these questions, the answer is obvious: only God is capable of perfect understanding.

In our age, we often hear the cry for understanding. Teenagers reacting against their parents scream, "You don't understand me!" Wives leaving their husbands in the midst of the liberation movement angrily accuse them, "You don't understand me!" Rebellion in the universities and violence in the high schools decry the lack of understanding on the part of school authorities. Every time I feel lonely, I think I am terribly misunderstood. To feel misunderstood and alone is a deep symptom of the alienation and estrangement of our times.

Into this picture comes the LORD. No one has to teach Him how to understand; in fact, He has known each of us from before our conception. He knows our personality traits, including all our foibles, and He is sensitive to our deepest needs. Long before we even speak them, He is aware of the desires of our hearts. He is conscious of all the twists and turns in our minds, all the patterns of our perceptions. Truly He understands us better than we do ourselves.

Why do we doubt then? When we turn to Him, why do we think we won't be completely understood? Don't we yet understand that He knows all the intricacies of our situations and will minister to all our very deepest needs?

We've all known people who are so supremely gifted in their chosen fields that it seems they never need to be taught. What they do best they do with such skill that it seems automatic. With seemingly no effort they concoct a fantastic gourmet dinner, shape a perceptive poem, or perform exquisitely a beautiful piece of music. Such tasks are easy for them because it is of their very nature to cook or to write or to sing. They freely give expression to their essential being.

Stretch that freedom now to infinity and apply it to our understanding of the character of our God. He does not need to be taught; everything comes naturally. How much more deeply could we ever be understood than by Him Whose very nature it is to understand? This is the impact of verse 14: we are made more aware that it is the very character of the LORD to know, to be just, to understand. What a tremendous security it is to realize that we are thoroughly understood by the One Who directs us (see v. 13). On the basis of His perfect wisdom and justice, He orders the affairs of our lives for our greatest benefit. Surely all things do work together for the good of those that love God — because He understands.

Working on this chapter has been a tremendous source of comfort for me personally. I have been struggling continually with the terrible tension of trying to keep all dimensions of my life in balance. I don't know how to be a servant of the church, a speaker, a student, and a human being all at once, and yet I do feel called to be each of them. Sometimes I get frustrated because I don't know any models, women with my professional interests or people with my particular struggles. Often I feel misunderstood by caring friends who try to help but just don't know all the factors that affect my decisions about how best to be a good steward of my time and abilities.

What peace is given to my spirit by the realization that my LORD knows and understands! If I am faithful in listening to the direction of His Spirit, He will create the proper balance and wholeness in my life. He will use me to serve others with all the fullness of His life in me. My Counselor has perfect insight into all that I am, because He is the One Who fashioned me. I long to experience His direction daily as I seek to be faithful to His calling.

I long to be more attentive to that Counselor. And I pray that the words of this chapter have stirred in you, too, a desire to trust more fully the perfect understanding of Him Who needs no one to teach Him or give Him counsel. He does indeed know all that is right and best.

The slogans that men devise, on the other hand, deceive us. The lifestyles promoted by the culture that encroaches upon us betray us. If we depend on human enlightenment, we will travel a dead-end street. Any humanistic rejection of God's answers will prove disastrous for us.

This fourteenth verse of Isaiah 40 teaches us Who this God is Whose answers we dare not reject. Its rhetorical questions confront us with the folly of our blind assumption that God is not able to handle all our needs. "Did God need to consult anyone for His enlightenment?" the prophet asks.

He Who needs no one to teach Him or to give Him counsel longs to be gracious to us (Isa. 30:18). How blessed we are if we reject the world's empty philosophies (Col. 2:8) and learn from Him (Matt. 11:29)!

QUESTIONS FOR FURTHER MEDITATION:
1. What things don't I understand about myself?
2. How does it help me to know that God knows and understands everything?
3. What other passages from God's Word show me that He understands?
4. What is the difference between the justice of the world and the justice of the LORD?
5. How does my faith help me to adjust to the rapid proliferation of knowledge in my culture?
6. What is the place of Christian counseling if the LORD Himself is our Counselor?
7. What does it mean to be truly enlightened?

The Cry of Finitude 15

*"Behold, the nations are like a drop from a bucket,
and are accounted as the dust on the scales;
behold, he takes up the isles like fine dust."*

Isaiah 40:15

"I just can't get the very last drop!" Whether we're trying to pour oil from a can, juice from a pitcher, or water from a bucket, that last drop usually just won't come. It's too tiny. Not enough remains to gather itself together to pour over the side. It just doesn't weigh enough to make it over the lip of the container. Finally, we give up. That last drop is inconsequential anyway.

That is the picture Isaiah uses to describe the nations. They are as a drop hanging from the lip of the bucket. With the same word that he chose to introduce the Lord GOD in verses 9 and 10, he cries, "Behold, the nations." The Hebrew noun is very much like the Greek word *ethnos* (from which we get *ethnic*). It means "the people" and carries connotations of peoples apart from the chosen people, Gentiles as contrasted with Jews. It can signify political entities, but it does not necessarily stress their governments as does our modern word *nations*.

The uniqueness of the image Isaiah selects to describe the nations is underscored by his deliberate choice of rare words. The word translated "drop" is used only here in the entire Old Testament; the word rendered "bucket" is used elsewhere only once, in Numbers. The phrase is introduced by a word of comparison and reads literally, "like a drop from a bucket," with the connotation of hanging. *The Jerusalem Bible* gives us a graphic version with its translation, "like a drop on the pail's rim."

The poetic parallel of the second line makes the nations even smaller. "As a fine dust on the balance they are reckoned." We just blow that dust away. It is of no account. And if some of it remains

83

on the scales, it won't matter anyway. The dust is too fine to distort the weighing.

"Behold," Isaiah says again, "the islands are so small that the LORD lifts them up as if they were pulverized." The verb here is closely related in sound to another verb that means to cast or to hurl; perhaps a pun is intended. God can pick up the coastlands as if they were fine powder. He might as well hurl them again into the sea. That might have been the way they were created. If the pun is intended, it's a good joke. The point of the whole verse is that nations and peoples who think they are important are really of no account in relation to the sovereignty of the Lord GOD. The message is not vindictive or vengeful; it merely illustrates again the majesty of the LORD.

This verse seems to be almost more appropriate in our time than it was in Isaiah's, because today there is such an emphasis on nations. We see constantly a fulfillment of the prophecy that Jesus made that "nation shall rise against nation." Newspapers and television newscasts report the subduing of nations, the termination of nations, the revolt of nations against their rulers or civil wars that rip apart nations, the accusations of nations one against another, and sometimes, rarely, the seeking of peace between nations.

Nations think they are very important, but toward this world scene the words of Isaiah are just as powerful as they were in his time. After all, he declares, the nations are only like a drop on the lip of a bucket in relation to the LORD. The statement is prefaced with the word *Behold!* as if to say, "Pay attention to this!" We had better sit up and take notice.

What a tremendous word of warning and what a powerful word of comfort this verse can give! First we should consider its warning. Different peoples today oftentimes get very proud about their nations. In the United States, for example, we have vast resources at our disposal. We have many great minds and willing workers to use and develop those resources. The problem is, however, that we begin to rely upon the strength of the nation and its weapons systems rather than upon the strength of the LORD. It seems that we, too, could get carried away easily into a captivity, physically or emotionally or spiritually. Perhaps we are already captive.

The Children of Israel at the time of Isaiah were very proud; they were quite confident of their own capabilities as a nation and of the fact that they were the Chosen People. But soon that confidence was brought low by the siege of Sennacherib, and later that confidence was destroyed as the Israelites were taken away into exile. We in the United States must also beware lest the power we depend upon in worldwide affairs is suddenly shown to be an illusion. Loss of respect for our nation has accompanied all the tragic events and the lack of morality in our government during the last few years, and distrust and antagonism have resounded throughout the world.

I especially saw the failure of the United States to be the power it expects to be when I was on concert tour around the world several years ago. In many nations that we visited in the Orient, the Middle East, and Europe, I was astounded at the hatred with which Americans were greeted. It was only after learning a few fragments of sentences in their languages, and only when I walked away by myself to meet the cities, that I was able to get a better understanding of the peoples we visited. Before that, their hostility against a tour group of Americans was overwhelming. I wanted to communicate, to learn, to share, to become a friend. What gave rise to their angry reaction?

It seemed they had experienced so many terrible tourists with all their pride and gluttony, their condescension and haughtiness, that they suspected all Americans of having similar attitudes toward them. I don't blame them. I didn't see much concern and love on the part of many tourists either, and at times I was ashamed of the insensitivity and materialism that I caught in myself.

Many tourists had such an active condescension because they felt themselves superior and deserving of every respect and service. That kind of pomposity must be brought low by this realization: "Behold, the nations are like a drop from the bucket; they are counted as the dust on the scales." God easily brushes off the dust from the scales so that His justice can be cleanly weighed.

I am not an alarmist or a pessimist or a cynic, but I do think that at all times Christians of every nation must evaluate their position and attitudes and recognize that, as God's family, we dare not put our trust in the peoples of this world. We have learned from previous verses that "all flesh is grass." Nations shall pass away. They are as easily cast aside as dust.

On the other hand, this verse also contains a tremendous word of hope, especially in this time of racial, political, and religious tensions among various peoples of the world. When we are fearful of communist invasions, of the pride of those governments that would demolish us, of the threat of nuclear annihilation or environmental deterioration, it is a great comfort to remember that those nations who are our enemies are also like a drop in a bucket. God truly is master over all nations; He has power to prevent our destruction.

That confidence, however, gives rise to a theological problem that I will raise briefly here but leave to other writers to answer: If God is in control, why did He not prevent the takeover of Viet Nam? Why does He not bring an end to the terrible conflicts that are now happening in many parts of the world? At this time I think particularly, and prayerfully, of civil strife in South Africa, the brutality in Uganda, the religious and political animosities in the Muslim world, and the constant threat of strife in so many other places of tension. These examples from the particular time at which I am writing are not unusual, of course; the situation has been the same throughout history, and will undoubtedly continue to be so.

An entirely different set of nations might be at odds with each other or threatening our national security by the time you read this, but Isaiah's message still applies. The LORD lifts up the isles (and continents, if necessary) as if they were fine powder. We can find hope, no matter what the world situation, in the fact that God is indeed sovereign. The nations are merely a drop on the pail's rim in relation to Him. In Him we must place our trust, not in governments, nor in weapons, nor in resources, nor in peoples or nations.

QUESTIONS FOR FURTHER MEDITATION:
1. At what times has my nation experienced a revival in its awareness of its inconsequentiality in relation to God, and what has happened during those times?

2. How can I be influential in changing the attitudes of my nation about itself?

3. What should be my country's attitude toward other nations?

4. What attitudes should control my behavior when I am a guest of other peoples?

5. How has the LORD's hand been seen in various conflicts throughout the course of world history?

6. How have nations been brought to their knees by the action of the LORD?

7. How can I help others to find their "national security" in the LORD rather than in the princes or weapons of this world?

The Cry of Meagerness 16

*"Lebanon would not suffice for fuel,
nor are its beasts enough for a burnt offering."*
                                             Isaiah 40:16

A million baby trees in three greenhouses! They look like
a carpet of inch-high grass. But imagine what they will be like in
eighty years when they forest part of a mountain top.

The Department of Natural Resources (DNR) for the State of
Washington has its greenhouses here in Olympia. The workers
plant the seeds in carrot-sized containers so that their roots can
wrap around the soil; thus the greenhouse trees can be used for
reforestation late in the summer or after a forest fire. Because of
the DNR's work, I have a much better appreciation for the vast
number of cedar trees that must have clothed Lebanon. I have
seen how much time and effort it takes to raise the trees to cover
just a small section of land.

Isaiah pokes fun at the inadequacy of all offerings to the LORD
by an indirect reference to the trees of Lebanon. His comments
are elliptical: "Lebanon not enough for burning; its beasts not
enough for a burnt offering." This is such a tangible picture of the
insufficiency of man's sacrifice. Consider the country of Lebanon,
how it was known far and wide for its beautiful cedars, how its
people had contributed vast treasures of their precious wood for
Solomon's building of the temple and his palaces. Yet all the wood
of that entire nation would not suffice for fuel for the offering God
deserves. The *Today's English Version* says, "The trees of
Lebanon are too few to even kindle the fire." Furthermore, all the
beasts that must have resided in those forests are vastly inadequate to make a burnt offering fit to honor the LORD.

This verse has profound and painful implications for each of us as individuals and for our churches collectively. Truly in this age of evangelical awareness, we understand that worship of God is not sacrifice, that our sacrifices cannot earn His favor, and yet how often it seems we suddenly believe — deceiving ourselves — that our pious efforts can gain God's grace. We get so falsely religious that we assume God's blessings must be poured out upon us more richly because of the immensity of our sacrifices.

An awesome contradiction exists between, on the one hand, the realization that we are saved by faith alone and, on the other hand, the need to justify our existence before God. In the first case, our desire to please God is a *response* to His grace. In the second, our sacrifices are an attempt to *prove* our love for Him. How hard it is for us to accept God's grace as freely as it is given! It hurts our egos to admit that all we are and all we do is made possible by God's action within us, and that never can we do anything out of our own strength to please Him.

Blaise Pascal understood an important truth when he said in his *Pensées* that the Old Testament sacrifices were not sufficient or pleasing to God, because at the time they were offered they both fulfilled and did not fulfill God's wishes. When the Children of Israel lost all sight of their personal relationship with their covenant God and resorted instead to meaningless multiplication of sacrifices, their offerings could not fulfill His desire for their love and faithfulness. God's holiness and justice caused Him to react with righteous wrath and indignation.

When will we learn this principle, that God does not require burnt offerings and sacrifices, but He looks for contrite and diligent hearts? Isaiah and many other Old Testament prophets emphasize constantly that God is not pleased with empty mechanics. They criticize the people of Israel severely for their hypocritical sacrifices, their phony offerings of gifts from the hands, but not from the heart. This verse adds the assertion that even the greatest sacrifices are puny anyway in comparison with the majesty of God and the size of offerings He deserves. Elsewhere in the book, Isaiah describes the sacrifices that God does desire: sacrifices of praise and rejoicing, the heart's gifts of commitment and trust, offerings of justice and compassion. What He desires is our very selves. What He wants is a willingness, a devotion, a trust, a submissiveness. He wishes that we would love Him with all our heart and soul and mind and strength.

The outcome of that kind of love, of course, is that all the rest of our being is directed properly besides. Then we make the right sacrifices. We do indeed burn up our Lebanons and offer all the animals therein. But the motive is different. It is not an attempt to be sufficient. Rather, it is the realization that there is no better use of Lebanon or her animals than to offer them in praise to God.

This gives rise to the whole painful question of our stewardship — of our talents and treasures, of our time and trust. How do we use our abilities? Too often we get pious and think that the best stewardship is to spend ourselves for our churches, when maybe God would have us use our skills to fight famine, to secure justice in the world, to raise godly children, or to give quietly and reverently a defense to those who ask us to account for the hope that lies within us (1 Pet. 3:15).

What about our treasures? Do our offerings to our churches only buy organs and stained glass windows and new shrubs for the landscaping, or are our financial resources being used for the spreading of the Kingdom of God, the offering of salvation to those who are lost, of food to those who are hungry, and of comfort to those without hope? I'm not opposed to pipe organs; I love to play them myself. And I'm not opposed to beautiful furniture and vestments and other signs and symbols of our adoration. Those are good aids to worship, assistants for fixing our minds on God. But have our luxurious buildings with all their gorgeous accouterments become places of pride instead of houses of worship? Do we realize that any percentage of our income is not enough for our offering? God wants 100 percent of our money; all of it should be used to glorify Him. It is hard to justify the way we spend the other 90 percent of our income when people are starving both physically and spiritually. Is our lifestyle in keeping with the One Who called us to sell our possessions and give to the poor?

Sometimes the offering of time is the biggest snare for church professionals. It is easy for us just to put in our time, to do our duties because that is our job. All the animals of Lebanon, all our Bible studies and counseling sessions and council meetings and hospital visitations, are not sufficient to honor the LORD. He wants every moment. We are to practice His presence even when we're not playing our professional parts.

Perhaps all our stewardship can be summed up in the word *trust*. God's desire is for us to surrender all to Him and trust His guidance for our way and His provision for all our needs. The sacrifice of Jesus was acceptable to the Father to atone for the sins of the whole world because it was based on a simple trust in the Father's plan for salvation. Our offerings are a response to that gift of Himself. We are to follow His model of dependent submission.

In the context of Isaiah's series of rhetorical questions challenging the believer to behold the power and might of God, we can't help but fall humbly to our knees in recognition that we could never even begin to offer anything that is worthy to praise His majestic name. Only in the confession of our feebleness, only in the realization of the destitution of our sacrifices, can we come humbly into the presence of the mighty God and know our proper place before Him.

This verse carries us back to the scene of Isaiah 6, wherein the prophet is confronted with the glory and majesty of God, high and lifted up on His throne, with His splendor filling the temple. Isaiah's only response could be the confession, "Woe is me! For I am lost; for I am a man of unclean lips." The only response we can make to the holiness of God is to recognize our desperation also. Then, when he had been cleansed, Isaiah could commit himself to the Lord's call for someone to go, with the consecration, "Here am I! Send me."

Let us also offer the sacrifice of our talents and treasures, our time and our trust — tokens of our response to the good news of the Lord's grace. We rejoice with the poet and sing,

> "Were the whole realm of nature mine, that were a tribute
> far too small.
>   Love so amazing, so divine, demands my soul, my life, my
> all."

I want to add, *"shall have* my soul, my life, my all!"

QUESTIONS FOR FURTHER MEDITATION:
1. Is there any place for sacrifice in the Christian faith, and, if so, what can I offer?

2. What is the value of giving up something for Lent or other such sacrifices?

3. If God doesn't need my sacrifices, am I free to go and do as I want? Why or why not?

4. What is the place of offerings gathered in worship services?

5. What is the meaning of the phrase, "sacrifice of praise?"

6. What is the value of fasting and prayer as an offering?

7. What are the good and bad points of my church's stewardship program?

The Cry of Emptiness 17

*"All the nations are as nothing before him,
they are accounted by him as less than
nothing and emptiness."*

Isaiah 40:17

It's hard to keep up with the map of the world these days.
Every year, new nations are formed and others are conquered and
wiped out of existence. Regardless of our positions on the war, we
watched with agony when South Viet Nam was crushed, and we
grieve over the state of many of the boat refugees who are being
turned away from country after country. Nations fearful of jeop-
ardizing their present political position consider the refugees
people who are good for nothing but trouble.

"Good for nothing," "less than nothing" — these are phrases
that we use to describe something that is meaningless, someone
who has no worth. It is painful to be called "less than nothing."
We all need to find value in ourselves. Yet that is how Isaiah
sternly characterizes the nations as he takes us beyond their
minuteness as shown in verse 15 to their complete emptiness in
the verse before us.

"All the nations as not," verse 17 begins literally. The word for
"not" is the same that was used twice in verse 16, but here it is
not followed by the word *enough*. The comparison is significant.
Although the forests of Lebanon are not sufficient and her beasts
are not adequate to prepare a suitable sacrifice to honor God,
there is the implication of at least some value in the phrase "not
enough." Here in verse 17, on the other hand, the nations have no
value. Before the LORD they are "as not."

The extended poetic parallel makes the judgment more severe.
It says literally, "They are reckoned to Him as less than zero and
without form." The verb is the same one used in verse 15, "they

95

are accorded," or "reckoned," although now the phrase "to Him" is added. The final word rendered "vanity" or "meaningless" or "emptiness" in various translations is the same Hebrew word that is used in Genesis 1:2 to describe the earth as "without form" and void.

The emphasis for this verse, which takes us beyond the message of verse 15, is this concept of emptiness, of vanity. *The Living Bible* paraphrases this verse in these words: "All the nations are as nothing to him; in his eyes they are less than nothing — mere emptiness and froth." The word *froth* is a graphic description of the concept we are about to explore.

Froth on the top of a glass of something is usually composed of bubbles, easily blown away, tasting only like air, not providing any substance. In the same way the nations are ephemeral, are easily conquered or destroyed, have no meaning, and do not provide a basis for security or the foundation for a happy life. It is important for us to recognize the totality of their meaninglessness.

What is it that makes a nation a nation? What enables nations to arise? Why do people rejoice in their heritage? What causes people to be willing to die for their country? All these dimensions illustrate the importance of nations. Why does Isaiah assert that they have no value?

For a while it was the fad in the United States to have bumper stickers that said, "America: Love It or Leave It!" Such a statement insists that people should think about that choice. Citizens were asked either to be responsible, as the bumper sticker owners defined responsibility, or to give up their citizenship. The situation that caused the prevalence of that bumper sticker was that many people were strongly questioning the government and criticizing its foreign policies. In reaction, many other people urged the critics either to change their minds or change their homeland.

Christians who recognize that this world is not their home must also wrestle with the question of citizenship. When we love the LORD and seek to be devoted to Him, what does it mean to sing "I Love America?" What is a proper perspective on patriotism?

I'm not going to outline a Christian stance on the value of

nationalism. I'm not going to advocate loving America or leaving it. But I do want to stir up in us radical thinking about the relative values of things. By radical I mean getting to the root of the matter, thinking critically about the perspective that Isaiah proposes.

I have experienced some moments of deep love for my country. Two stand out in my memory and provide some lessons related to this verse.

First, I'll never forget the Fourth of July that I spent in Vellore, India. As indicated in chapter 15, much of our concert tour around the world brought great distress to me and shame about my homeland, but Independence Day provided a positive impression. I'll never forget the tears that flowed during the concert when our choir sang first the Indian national anthem and then our own. And what fun we had when the students of the Christian Medical College set off fireworks to help us celebrate. I was dressed in a sari at that party and had eaten Indian food for dinner, but the concert had stirred up my love for my homeland. My heart overflowed with thanks to God for all the blessings and the liberty of my homeland and the courage of the people who had fought and still fight that she could be free.

Second, I'll never forget the joy of seeing the United States flag when we flew into an airport in Israel. Amidst all the strange experiences and the hostilities we had encountered in our travels, the flag reminded me that at home I felt at home. I often long for that same sense of belonging now when I view the flag at parades many years later.

Both of those experiences speak of something deeper than the surface impressions. The first occasion meant so much to me because, in spite of my generally critical attitude toward the culture of my homeland, that night I caught sight of the LORD's presence there. My gratitude arose because I finally recognized that what gave meaning to any sort of patriotism was the awareness that a nation, too, is nothing without the LORD.

The second experience impressed me so deeply because, contrary to my expectation at that time, I didn't feel at home when I returned home. As we flew into New York City, I remember feeling aghast at all the swimming pools, huge cars, boats, and exclusive homes I saw. Somehow I couldn't reconcile American materialism and luxury with the grinding poverty, the famine and the death that I had witnessed in the Orient and India. Since then I have never felt at home in my homeland. Somehow our wealthy culture seems out of joint. The homelessness I feel reminds me that I am made for another world (see chap. 6).

Those are two implications of Isaiah's message in verse 17: that nations are nothing before the LORD except as they are with the LORD, and that they are meaningless as we recognize our purposeful heritage elsewhere.

We lose sight of the fact that our heritage here on earth is not our primary heritage. I am, above all, a stranger, an alien. I am a sojourner and an ambassador here. It is good to be grateful for the land that is my home. It is good to recognize my nation's strong points and to be grateful for her resources, but it is dangerous to live entirely for the sake of my country. It is absurdity to commit my life to froth.

It is not wrong to love or to serve our country. The problem arises when we make the nation or our people our god, when we give them a misplaced esteem and priority in our lives.

Unfortunately, our nation seems to have lost sight of her original pledge to be "one nation under God." The emphasis of God's sovereignty over our land is no longer considered relevant. For that reason I cannot give undivided loyalty to my country. I have to be critical of its morality and governmental policies, its consumerism and waste, when they are opposed to what I believe God would have us do and be as loving citizens of His Kingdom.

Augustine fully understood the meaning of this verse that nations are as nothing before the LORD when he wrote his famous *The City of God*. In that important work, he contrasted earthly kingdoms with the heavenly kingdom and recognized that Christians are citizens of both at the same time. We can't become so heavenly minded that we are no earthly good, as the saying goes. We are to be good citizens of the earthly kingdom while we are here. What enables us to be the best possible citizens, however, is our awareness that our primary heritage is our citizenship in a greater kingdom. We sing, "I'm but a stranger here; heaven is my home." Perhaps that is the best lesson we can derive from this verse as we recognize the meaninglessness of nations apart from God.

QUESTIONS FOR FURTHER MEDITATION:
1. If nations are meaningless, what is the value of citizenship in a particular one?
2. What is the purpose of a nation?
3. What is the meaning of my citizenship in heaven?
4. How can I draw the line between proper earthly citizenship and a distortion of it?
5. With what sort of perspective can I best serve my nation?
6. How can I avoid failure in my responsibility to be a good citizen?
7. How can I become more aware of my heavenly citizenship in the mundane affairs of daily life in the earthly sphere?

The Cry of Incomparability 18

"To whom then will you liken God,
or what likeness compare with him?"
Isaiah 40:18

I watched with horror as the salesman sprinkled a packet of dirt on my carpet. Then he challenged me to try to pick it up with the ancient vacuum cleaner I was borrowing. After I'd finished, he used his product to go over the same area of floor a few times. When he opened his cleaner's bag, I was astounded at all the dirt we found there. I couldn't deny the evidence. His product was so very much better that I was glad to pay the extra price to invest in such a good cleaner.

"It's the real thing!" "Why settle for less?" "We know what you're looking for." Such advertising slogans urge us to compare products and discover that the particular one being advertised is really the best. They imply that we will, of course, recognize the vast superiority of the particular product at hand.

Isaiah does somewhat the same thing in this verse (although his claims about God are obviously infinitely more reliable than advertisers' claims). The prophet asks the penetrating question, "To whom will you liken God?" The form of the question, though, is terribly ironic and, consequently, more piercing.

To create the irony, Isaiah chooses an unusual word, the name *el*, for God. Usually in the Old Testament the plural form *Elohim* or the name *el* with another name attached (like *Shaddai* — "almighty") is used to designate Yahweh. Here *el* stands alone as His name.

El was originally the name of the Canaanite chief deity, who seems to have been retired somewhat to a figurehead position with the advent of Baal worship. In the context of this chapter,

101

with its comments about Lebanon, the coastlands (perhaps a reference to the Greek isles, with all their conflicting deities), and the dusty nations, Isaiah's choice implies a sarcasm. *Elohim* is the real God. To compare anything to the real God reduces Him to a mere figurehead, to less than the God that He is — in short, to *el.* The LORD is the only real God. All the rest are fakes and shams, mere pretenders to the throne.

The irony is reinforced by the verb choice in the poetic parallel, which says, "Or what image will you compare to Him?" The specific verb, "to compare," implies the result of arranging or setting forth, perhaps in battle array against the thing compared. The connotation, then, is that those who set false deities in opposition to God discover that no image can even begin to compare to His power, His sovereignty, or all that He is.

This verse seems to be a focus in the midst of the fortieth chapter. It helps us to understand all the chapter's rhetorical questions about the majesty and sovereignty of God. All the main themes of the chapter evolve from this basic point: nothing — not flesh, nor idols, nor nations — can compare with the LORD. *The Living Bible* says, "How can we describe God?" And *The Jerusalem Bible* adds, "What image could you contrive of him?"

Those very significant questions ought also to be the focus of our existence. How can we describe God? By what means shall we come to a greater awareness of Him? Isaiah's biting sarcasm forces us to realize that the way we describe God or the false deities that we array against Him indicates our misunderstanding of His character.

The implications of this verse for our lives move in two divergent directions. First, the questions criticize the way we reduce God by making Him *el* instead of *Elohim*, by setting false images against Him. Second, the verse implies that we should gain a proper perspective on God, and thus it encourages us to formulate rightly our descriptions of Him. (Our negative reductions will be considered more thoroughly in the next chapter.)

On the positive side, this verse urges us to increase our appreciation for all that God is by enlarging our vocabulary about Him. The way we perceive Him will affect how we come to Him. If we describe Him as a loving father and picture Him with tenderness and gentleness, we will turn to Him as trusting children. But if we perceive Him only as a harsh judge, we will be afraid of Him, and we will not turn to Him in our needs. So Isaiah asks the very crucial question, "To whom then will you liken God?"

Obviously, the answer is that we cannot compare anyone to Him. There is nothing that comes close to corresponding to Him. We cannot even group together many, many factors and come up with a good composite picture. God is too much larger than that.

The challenge before us as Christians is to explore the nature of God as deeply as we can in order to proclaim that nature more accurately. We want to begin to grasp some of the characteristics by which He has made Himself known. One of the purposes for our Bible studies and quiet times should be to add and add and add to our understanding of what God is like.

The entire quest of theology can be summarized in these two words: "Know God!" We cannot quickly dismiss Him with a single picture and think we have understood Who He is. Instead, as we seek to compare Him, as we try to draw His likeness in the positive sense, we must make use of many, many different pictures put together if we are to perceive Him a bit more adequately (and still we must realize that we grossly understate His infinite character).

That is one of the reasons we need four gospels to give us four different perspectives on the character of Jesus, and still the evangelist John concludes, "But there are also many other things which Jesus did; were every one of them to be written, I suppose that the world itself could not contain the books that would be written" (John 21:25). One of the greatest joys in my work is that no matter how many times I lead Bible studies on a particular section of the Scriptures, that same passage will always unlock new Truth for me about the nature of God.

One of the essential reasons for the Body of Christ is that it takes all of God's people to show us everything He wants to tell us about Himself. Consequently, Peter urges us in his first letter to be good stewards of that which has been given to us, employing our gifts for one another and revealing, by our stewardship, the many-sided grace of God (1 Pet. 4:11).

God's grace is so large that we just cannot begin to fathom its immensity. We observe parts of His character in many different forms. For example, as I write these words I'm thinking about an incident that happened yesterday. My car stalled on the freeway because my malfunctioning gas gauge indicated I still had ⅜ of a tank, when actually I was out of gas. I coasted off an exit ramp and reached the bottom of the hill. Not knowing what was wrong, I was quite frightened. Being terribly unmechanical, I had no idea how to begin to figure out what was wrong. However, just when I was about to panic, two young gentlemen stopped, offered to help, pushed until I could get the car started by popping the clutch, and so enabled me to get going again. I was able to travel just far enough to coast finally to a safe place. A friend loaned me her car for the rest of the day until I could get gas for mine.

Those three individuals revealed to me several dimensions of the grace of God. The fact that the Father had provided their assistance just at the time of my frantic need was an appropriate picture of how full His provision for us is. The fact that they helped so willingly and so gently, probably sensing both my frustration and my fear, was another picture of God's tender care. I needed to add both pictures to my collage of understanding.

Each day we add dimensions to our comprehension of the character of God, always knowing that our perception is still inadequate. Today I saw His bounty in raspberry fields as I discovered that He had provided plenty for me, plenty for all the other pickers, and plenty for the birds, with still some left over to be sure. What a lovely picture of God's grace — always overflowing.

I also saw God's compassion today in a person with whom I had a Bible study exploring the concept of death. Together we realized also that the Father is on the other side of death and waiting to receive us.

Many things, people, and incidents give us bits and pieces for our growing knowledge of the character of God — not that they ARE God, but that His creatures reveal their Creator. Above all, He is to be found in His Word. When we try to compare Him or describe Him or draw an image of Him, we find that nothing will do. God cannot be contained. We dare not put Him into boxes and think we have comprehended Him. And yet we do catch glimpses of His character, primarily through His Word and through other gifts He has given us. Some day we shall know Him face to face, and then, at last, our descriptions will be accurate.

Of course, Isaiah is directing his remarks particularly against the folly of those who make images of God (as we will see in the next verse), but his words force us to recognize also the inadequacy of all our perceptions of God. To begin to learn how powerful and mighty He is, how infinite — how we are just beginning to get acquainted — surely will result in our hearts being stirred up to seek after Him more diligently. To know God as He has revealed Himself to us gives us enough to do for a lifetime, and an eternity besides.

QUESTIONS FOR FURTHER MEDITATION:
1. To what false gods do I frequently turn?
2. What kinds of situations cause me to turn away from God?
3. How do I make my God too small?
4. What are my favorite pictures of God?
5. What new dimensions of God's character have I learned about in the past few days?
6. How have I experienced His love in a special way today?
7. How can my church serve to expand my understanding of God's character?

The Cry against Idolatry 19

"The idol! a workman casts it,
and a goldsmith overlays it with gold,
and casts for it silver chains."
Isaiah 40:19

I was horrified! They had mummified a girl alive to put her inside the Buddha statue. "That is how we give the image a spirit," our guide explained. I learned later that every image of Buddha has the spirit of some creature buried alive inside, whether it be that of a fly or a person. The craftsman's work is not complete until the spirit is given to his idol.

Such care is taken by a craftsman who makes an idol, who tries to make a god. Isaiah pokes fun in this verse particularly at those who think that God can be constructed by a craftsman. What folly, he implies, to think that something made with man's hands, something decorated by an artisan, could be compared to God. Even though it might be overlaid with the most precious of metals, it is still man-made.

The humor of the picture is reinforced by the construction of the Hebrew phrases in this verse. Usually the subject or verb of the sentence comes first; putting the direct object at the beginning, as Isaiah does here, is done for special emphasis. Thus, the first phrase literally reads, "The idol! a craftsman casts."

The second phrase adds that "a smith with the gold overlays it." Then the third phrase doesn't even have a verb. The word for "smith" is now found in a participial form to convey this addition: "and chains a silver smithing."

The purpose of those chains is unclear. Perhaps they are used to decorate the image. The statement of the following verse, urging that the idol be made skillfully so that it won't totter, might suggest that the chains mentioned here were used to fasten the image so it wouldn't fall down. If that is the intent, the last phrase doubly reinforces the idea of the ineffectiveness of man's construction. What image could ever be prepared to compare with the living God if it needs chains to hold it erect?

I am reminded of conversations with my very dear Taiwanese friend, who was a Buddhist before becoming a Christian. As a little boy, Chi Ping watched the idol craftsman make the Buddha, carving it with his tools, giving the statue eyes, shaping his mouth, forming the ears. Then, when his work was completed, someone took the image home, set it up on his altar, and used it for worship. Chi Ping was already haunted by this experience as a young person. He had observed the makers of idols as they carved the wood, and yet those idols assumed a prominent place in his home. Many years later he discovered that God is so much larger, and, with great Joy, he gave his life eagerly to Jesus Christ as his Savior and Lord.

This verse reinforces the criticism of the previous verse so that we will consider its negative side at this time and allow it to reprimand us. Isaiah was just in being sarcastic with the Israelites. To be swept into the worship of the false deities of their neighbors was sheer folly on their part. God had warned them that they must destroy the pagan influences that surrounded them, and He had proved Himself time and again to be faithful to His promises and powerful to care for His people. For the Children of Israel to reject such clear evidence was blindly ridiculous.

Lest we condemn them without due caution, however, we must realize that we all do the same thing. God has warned us, and He has proved Himself to us time and again — and yet, in blatant rejection or whimpering complaint, we turn away from Him to all sorts of false gods. We array against Him material pleasures, power and prestige, or the ambitions of this world (John's "the lust of the flesh and the lust of the eyes and the pride of life" — see 1 John 2:16), and never realize how ludicrous is the comparison.

I don't know what false gods you arrange, but I shudder to recognize the many I set forth. Every time I turn to another god, I reduce God and miss out on some of what He wants to be for me and to give to me. When I choose ease instead of struggle, I miss the ecstasy of victory. When I choose pleasure instead of pain, I miss the peace. When I crave affirmation from the world to boost my ego, I get hollow accolades that prevent me from hearing the true sense of worth that God confers.

We worship the products of our hands, things we have overlaid with gold or molded in a base of silver and then set up to worship. We can make so many things into idols without pausing to realize they are the products of our hands. We commit our lives to them and invest all our wealth in them. We spend all our time crafting them and all our resources decorating them.

Notice how the workmen are pictured in this verse. A craftsman casts the idol carefully. The verb actually means "to pour out," so it might suggest the whole process of constructing a mold, refining the metal, and pouring it into the mold. Next a smith overlays it with gold; meanwhile, perhaps a silversmith is fashioning silver chains by which it can hang or be decorated. The idol is made beautiful. Much care is invested in its special crafting.

In such attempts at beautifying the idol, we see directly the work of the great deceiver. Satan hides the emptiness of our images under an overlay of gold. The apostle Paul comments that he is capable of disguising himself as an angel of light (2 Cor. 11:14), and in John 8:44, Jesus calls him the father of lies. So much of what we construct with our own hands — our power, our clothes, our homes and other possessions — is covered with beautiful gold to create the illusion of great value. Our task as God's people is to see the true value of things without their superficial layering of gold, to scratch beneath the surface to discover what things actually are.

What might particularly appeal to you? What to you is truly of value? When I stop to question myself, I am astounded at the triviality of the things that have become so important for me. It isn't that we shouldn't be good stewards of our things, nor that we shouldn't have or make beautiful things. But when those things are only seen for their gold exteriors, our sense of values is distorted. When we mistake things for ends in themselves and not merely tools for our existence, our priorities are confused.

My china is a good example. Because I am the oldest granddaughter on my mother's side, I was given Grandmother's china after her death. I received this gift with great gratitude, and, although I try to live as simply as I can, I treasure the beautiful china and use it frequently. To serve guests with the china reminds me of my grandmother and brings me close to my family. I also think it says something significant to my guests, telling them they are indeed very special, that I am using the best dishes to welcome them to my home.

If, however, that china becomes a god to me, its value has been distorted. I remember that once when a friend was drying a piece, I worried that he might break it. I was astonished at my own feelings. Something that is just made by a workman, even though overlaid with gold, should not become more important than my relationship with a friend.

In the same way, every time we make other objects the center of our attention, we have constructed an idol. How often do we get overly anxious about the things we possess lest anyone damage them or keep them too long, or use them improperly? We should take good care of the things God entrusts to us, but we ought not to overlay them with gold in our minds.

We must remember the difference between means and ends. Any time we make an object a goal to attain, it has become an idol. That sounds like an awfully strong statement, but I believe that it is what the Scriptures declare. We possess all things in trust, so that we might use them to serve the Lord.

We don't buy a house to own a beautiful house; it should not be the end in itself. Rather, we buy a house so that God's purposes for our families might be accomplished and His gift of hospitality extended.

Sometimes we let our very church buildings become overlaid with gold. We get so proud of their fine furnishings that we don't want to let outsiders from the community use the facilities for ministering efforts, such as meetings of Alcoholics Anonymous or a day-care center for senior citizens. Do the images of God in our churches entice us to worship them or aid us in focusing our attention on God?

This understanding of things does not mean the elimination of possessions or the ending of our pleasure. We must remember, however, that pleasure, too, is not an end. Our pleasure makes us happier, more attractive servants of the Lord. Everything we use is God's to own. We are grateful that He has so generously loaned us such wonderful means for His service.

QUESTIONS FOR FURTHER MEDITATION:

1. What are some things I have made into idols?

2. How can I perceive Satan's deception of casting things in gold to make them falsely appealing?

3. How can I be a successful image breaker without losing sight of those things that God gives me to enjoy and of which I ought to be a good steward?

4. How can I successfully use images to grow in my appreciation of God, without beginning to worship those images themselves?

5. How can I enjoy God's creation without having it take the place of the Creator in my worship?

6. How can my church help me to destroy the idols that distort my thinking?

7. How can I prevent my church buildings from also becoming deceptive idols?

The Cry of Impoverishment 20

*"He who is impoverished chooses for an offering
wood that will not rot;
he seeks out a skillful craftsman
to set up an image that will not move."*

Isaiah 40:20

You can't win either way. If someone asks, "Have you stopped beating your child?" either answer gets you in trouble. To say "Yes" means you were beating that child. To say "No" declares that you are still doing it. Isaiah sets up the same sort of dilemma from which there is no escape in verse 20. He wants to force the Israelites to confront the irrationality of their dependence on idols.

You can't win either way. You want to construct the idol securely enough so that it won't fall down. But when you make it that secure, you just reinforce the realization that it can't move at all to help you. What is the value of a nontottering image?

Once again the irony of the situation comes through strongly as Isaiah continues to describe man's efforts to make himself idols. His anguish over all the wasted effort is poignantly apparent. First, he contrasts those "too poor for a contribution" with the wealthy ones who could purchase the idols overlaid with gold and hung with silver (see v. 19). Although the poor cannot lavish such attention and cost on their images, they do their best, Isaiah notes. They at least are careful when they select their tree so that their idol can be made of wood that will not rot. They will do everything they can to make the idol last. But even the best wood cannot last forever. Ultimately, it, too, withers as the grass (see vv. 6-8).

Next, the poor choose a skillful craftsman, one who has the ability and technique to carve a fitting image. Above all, they want the craftsman to construct the idol so that it "shall not be moved" (KJV), a "sturdy image" (JB) that "will not totter" (NASB).

113

The irony is doubly reinforced in this last phrase by two word choices. To describe the action of the craftsman in constructing the idol, Isaiah chooses a verb that is used in the Old Testament to describe the "establishing" of kings, the heavens, or the faithfulness of God. The craftsman seeks to establish the idol as firmly as God fixed the mountains. He and the impoverished one who selected him want the idol to be made firm so that it cannot fall down. But what benefit to man can be brought by a god who was made by man? How vastly different it is when one's God is the One Who Himself established everything.

The final word choice of the verse stresses that the impoverished one and his craftsman want an idol that will not be shaken or moved. They don't want anything to knock over their god. What good can be done by such a god for whom such precaution must be taken? In fact, what good is a god who cannot be moved and who cannot move?

These two ideas together create a stark contrast. In man's efforts to establish an idol that is sturdy, he makes an idol that cannot move. A sturdy idol that cannot move is not capable of doing anything.

As I ponder this verse, I am reminded of the visit to the big Buddha in central Taiwan. Precaution was taken to protect the Buddha by various entrance monsters. I walked all over the grounds and surveyed the Buddha from every angle as I watched the people pray in hopelessness and dejection. All the while I was there, I kept hearing in my mind the words from Psalm 115:4-8 concerning idols that have ears but do not hear, that have mouths but cannot speak. There was the Buddha, a huge iron hulk, unable to do anything for the people who prostrated themselves before him. His hands could not reach out to heal or to comfort.

As we visited, I discovered that it is possible to go up inside his head, so I climbed to the top and looked out through his eyes. From that perspective, I was profoundly saddened as I saw the destitution of the neighboring countryside and the fatalistic approach of the worshiping peasants. They had little basis for hope, and this image could not give them any. No matter how skillful the craftsman that man selects, the images that are constructed and the false understandings of God that lie behind them cannot save or help.

The Living Bible underscores this inadequacy with its paraphrase, "The man too poor to buy expensive gods like that [v. 19] will find a tree free from rot and hire a man to carve a face on it, and that's his god — a god that cannot even move!"

Once again we learn that man's best efforts to choose and establish carefully result in futility and meaninglessness. The idol cannot move. We might think ourselves too cultivated or civilized to be accused by this verse, and yet I find it a profound observation of the hypocrisy of my life. Sometimes we don't even pretend to overlay our idols with gold or cast for them silver chains. Instead, out of our impoverishment we clutch frantically at anything that will do. We grasp for some sort of god to sustain us. For example, we might turn to an increase in salary or a promotion in power to find meaning in our jobs and lives.

The society around us seems lost in the mad dash to find some sort of god to believe in, something to live for, some purpose that will ease the longing of the *Sehnsucht* (see chap. 6). Sometimes we even make false gods out of the pretensions of our worship. Our making of idols to replace God is in vain. How easily the things of this world can become gods for us.

As I've been working on the revisions of this book, I'm facing some major changes in my life. These changes of work might necessitate a move to another city, and that makes me terribly insecure at the moment. I'm moving out of the office at the church I've been serving for three and one-half years, and I don't know for sure to what I'm moving. It is shocking for me to realize how much a home or office can become a god, and how desperately I need them not to totter. Something — anything! — must be secure when everything else around a person seems to be moving.

A final point to note is the totality of our failure and incapability when we consider this verse in relation to its context. We see both the futility of our man-made gods (in this verse and vv. 18 and 19) and the inadequacy of the offerings we bring (v. 16). There is the rebellion against God when we crave our own gods, and then there is His reaction to our attempts to make an offering or an image to worship — if not of gold and silver, then at least of wood that will not rot. Both the offering and the gods to whom we present it are nothing but vanity.

How different when we follow Jesus Christ! We don't choose a skillful craftsman, a master storyteller, to set up the image. Instead, we believe that God, THE Skillful Craftsman, has given us the uncreated image of Himself. He is the One begotten, but not made, and He offers Himself as the Offering. When we present Him Who is the Offering to Him Who is our God, we are totally justified. Only in the grace and merit of Jesus Christ are offering and God successfully brought together.

QUESTIONS FOR FURTHER MEDITATION:

1. When my life fails to produce silver and gold, to what do I turn?

2. When have I compromised my values and settled for lesser gods?

3. What kinds of skillful craftsmen, such as advertisers, set up idols to which I turn?

4. How can I observe that my gods are not able to move?

5. Why do I turn to other gods in the first place?

6. What sorts of things keep people from turning away from their false gods?

7. How could I be helpful in leading people away from gods that can't move?

The Cry to Know and Hear 21

"Have you not known? Have you not heard?
Has it not been told you from the beginning?
Have you not understood from the foundations of the earth?"
Isaiah 40:21

Why couldn't she remember where to stand on the volleyball court? I had told her so many times how to figure out where her position should be when the opponents were serving, and yet we consistently lost points because she wasn't in place to return the serve. She should have been able to guess her place just by noticing everyone else's position on the court. And we'd been telling her about the set-ups ever since she first started playing with us. She ought to have understood them by now! Hadn't she been listening?

Isaiah also wonders if anyone has been listening as he asks a painful set of questions with a tone of exasperated impatience. We are challenged by the prophet to realize that we ought to know better; that we should have paid better attention when we could have heard; that we might have been listening more when things were first told us at the beginning; that we could have understood from the very fact of creation itself. We have no excuse.

Each phrase in this verse begins with a form that combines the interrogative with a word that means "not." Thus, the verse keeps saying, "Do you not?" "Do you not?" as if to ask, "Well, why don't you?"

The first verb form is one of continuous action in the Hebrew. Isaiah asks, "Will you not know?," or "Are you not yet knowing?," as if to say, "Have you not figured it out yet so that you will not know?" The verb root is a repetition of the one that occurs in both verses 13 and 14 and again in 14 as a noun. Such frequent repetition there to state that no one can help God to know contrasts

117

sharply with the painful point here that man just does not yet recognize the truth.

"Will you not hear?" Isaiah continues. The phrase reminds us of the original message given to Isaiah when he was called (see Isa. 6). God told him to proclaim to the people, "Hearing, do not hear" (v. 9). The people's ears were dulled by their own rebellion. Again the verb is in an imperfect, or not-yet-completed, form. The question might be phrased, "Have you not yet come to hear?" or "Are you still not hearing?"

The third question of this verse asks in the Hebrew, "Has it not been told you from the head?" "The head" emphasizes the beginning or the first, of course, but it also seems to suggest the source. God Who is the Beginning One has revealed Himself from the start. In fact, as the final question asserts, we should have understood from the "foundations of the earth."

One element of controversy in the history of the church has been the question of whether there is such a thing as natural revelation in addition to God's exposition of Himself in His Word. This verse combines the two. It suggests natural revelation in the phrase "Have you not understood from the foundations of the earth?" A theology of God's revelation of Himself is implied by the phrase "Has it not been told you from the beginning?" In other words, God's disclosure of His character comes about both by what we observe and by what He has told us in His Word.

The four questions of this verse are not mere idle speculation. They are terribly indicting. *The Living Bible* paraphrases them, "Are you so ignorant? Are you so deaf to the words of God — the words he gave you before the worlds began? Have you never heard nor understood?" Why can't we comprehend God's messages? Don't we know? Haven't we been told? Can't we grasp what has been going on for a long time? It has been declared for us; why haven't we perceived?

The questions remind me of Jesus' words to His disciples in Mark 8. After two instances of feeding the multitudes (first the 5000 men plus women and children and then the 4000 plus), followed each time by discussion with the Pharisees and then the specific healing of an individual, Jesus asks the disciples who men say that He is. When they respond, "John or Elijah," He asks them what they think. Peter's confession, "You are the Christ," is the climax of the whole gospel account. Yet just prior to this conversation the disciples had been with Jesus in the boat. Worrying that they had no bread, they misunderstood Jesus' warning to them to avoid the leaven of the Pharisees.

Jesus rebukes them in words reminiscent of this verse from Isaiah. Piercingly, He questions them, "Do you not yet perceive or understand? Are your hearts hardened? Having eyes do you not see, and having ears do you not hear? And do you not remember?... Do you not yet understand? (Mark 8:17-18, 21).

These questions were leading to the declaration, "You are the Christ," but while in the boat the disciples did not yet understand Who He was and is. Even after making this glorious proclamation, Peter himself did not understand, and tried to talk Jesus out of His mission, as the Christ, to die (Mark 8:32).

Isaiah, more than any other Old Testament prophet, looked forward to the coming of the Christ, but he himself did not fully understand the Messiah about Whom he prophesied. He could not know the totality of the fulfillment of the Word he wrote. Yet he did perceive the character of his covenant God, and he expected God to continue fulfilling His promises and reigning majestically over the earth (see the next verse). Therefore, unknowingly, he anticipates Jesus and asks this same significant question: "Do you not yet understand?"

Why don't we understand? We don't know or hear or understand because we don't pay attention. Various problems divert our attention: our personal pride often gets in the way; we fail to recognize the kinds of promises God wants to keep for us; or we try to earn the grace that He wants to bestow freely. Many things obstruct our understanding.

One of the biggest obstructions is the simple fact that we neglect to make use of the means God has given us for growth in our understanding. He has given us His Word, and He told us that it alone stands forever. Yet we fail to read it, to study it, to meditate upon it, to "hide it in our hearts."

We have been conducting an experiment for more than a year now in the church I serve. The experiment stresses discipleship, and thirteen persons, including me, in two groups are diligently seeking to take seriously the opportunities God makes available for us to grow in our faith. We are having a difficult struggle.

As we seek to establish and improve our habits of "quiet time" and personal Bible study and prayer, we are encountering all kinds of obstructions. That is to be expected, of course, because the last thing in the world Satan wants to happen is for God's people to take seriously Jesus' command to search the Scriptures. Sometimes we encounter obstacles from the inside — little hurts and bad attitudes that have not been dealt with successfully. Sometimes we must surmount obstacles from the outside — people's criticism or mockery — in order to have the freedom to hear and understand.

If we as God's people have not known, perhaps it is because we have not paid much attention. If we have not heard, maybe it is because we have not taken advantage of opportunities to hear the Word of God being spoken. If we don't think it has been told us from the beginning, perhaps we have missed the telling, the revelation in the Word of God, because we have failed to open that Word and study it. If we have not understood from the foundations of the earth, too often it is because we make up other explanations for its beginning and lose sight of God's eternal plans. Above all, God desires to reveal Himself to His people. We fail to trust Him for His revelation because we do not yet understand that He is such a God of grace.

What do we do, then, with the indictments of this verse? We can react in one of two ways: one is from the Law; the other, from the gospel. If we take this verse as a word of Law, it is a word saying to us, "Shape up or ship out." If we can't manage sufficiently well this process of understanding, we might as well forget it and give up.

On the other hand, we can hear this Word as a message of gracious invitation, even though it is indicting. This indicting Word becomes, then, a Word of hope for us nonetheless. We have failed to hear and understand and know, but God's Word to us is forgiveness and not condemnation. He does not come to us with wrathful judgment against our ignorance and neglect. He comes to us with the merits of His Son and invites us to change that situation, beginning now. These words can serve as an inspiration to us to accept His forgiveness and grace and to let them free us to begin better to know, to pay more attention, to listen, to see.

God does indeed want to reveal Himself to us; if we're not growing in our knowledge of Him, it is never because He has not made such growth possible. If we fail to perceive His grace and to learn of His character, it is because we have failed to spend time with Him. What better motivation can there be for us to establish habits of quiet time and study?

It IS possible for us to know. It IS achievable for us to hear. Good news HAS been declared to us from the beginning. We WILL be able to understand. It's a matter of opening our eyes, ears, hearts, and minds — and Bibles.

QUESTIONS FOR FURTHER MEDITATION:

1. What means might I use to become better acquainted with the revelation of God?

2. How can I grow in my ability to listen when God speaks and understand what He says?

3. How can I apply these words to myself as invitation and not condemnation?

4. How can I make the knowledge of God a knowledge of the heart as well as of the head?

5. What do I do about passages in the Scriptures or revelations from God that I just cannot understand?

6. What is it exactly that I am supposed to know, hear, and understand?

7. What use can I make of this verse in my relationships with others?

The Cry of God's Dwelling 22

"It is he who sits above the circle of the earth,
and its inhabitants are like grasshoppers;
who stretches out the heavens like a curtain,
and spreads them like a tent to dwell in."
Isaiah 40:22

I'd have a terrible time pitching a tent. I've never done it by myself, and only rarely have I helped someone else do it. Besides that, as I admitted earlier, I'm terribly unmechanical and not very skilled at putting things together.

The Bedouins of the Middle East, on the other hand, set up their tents with ease. They have lived in them all their lives, traveling from one place to another according to the seasons and available work. To spread out a tent is for them a very simple operation.

Just as easily as the Bedouins put up a tent, Isaiah proclaims, the LORD spread out the heavens. After his mockery of the idol makers and his rebuke of those who should know but have not heard and do not understand, the prophet returns to his theme of the majesty and sovereignty of God. Again he compares God to man and notes the giant discrepancy.

This verse revolves around the concept of dwelling. That concept occurs in the first two lines as a participle, the first time in a singular form referring to God's "dwelling upon the vault of the earth." The second time it's a plural to identify "its [the earth's] dwelling ones," who are, in comparison to God, "like grasshoppers." The word translated "vault", or "circle" in the first line comes from a verb meaning "to draw around" or "to make a circle." Hence, it might signify the horizon of the earth; but more likely in this context it means a sphere or vault, the dome of the earth's sky. God reigns majestically from the throne of the heavens. In stark contrast, those dwelling under that dome are as grasshoppers — small, insignificant, noisy, perhaps even pesty.

Finally, the concept of dwelling occurs again as an infinitive in the last poetic couplet, when Isaiah describes God as "stretching the heavens out like a curtain and spreading them out like a tent to dwell in." The word translated "tent" in the last phrase signifies a normal Bedouin tent, used from before the time of Abraham and still observable in the Middle East today.

Once again, anthropomorphic images (i.e., using human characteristics to describe God) are chosen so that we can begin to grasp the infinity of God. The first set of parallel lines continues the theme of God's greatness introduced earlier in Isaiah's fortieth chapter. The pictures suggest God's providential upholding and maintaining of the universe. They give us another glimpse of His sovereign care. We look up at the wide expanse of sky and realize that God, sitting above it, holds it up.

Scientists can tell us how incredibly crucial the earth's atmosphere is. We all know that it is the vault of heaven that enables life to exist as it does on planet earth. It is comforting to know that God is the One Who is in control of that vault. He rules from His throne upon it to allow the temperatures to be tolerable and the amount of moisture to be sufficient, to prevent collisions with other planets and meteors. So much is entailed in God's sitting enthroned above the vault of heaven!

Once I saw a "Twilight Zone" television episode in which many of the people of the world were moving north because the planet was getting so hot. According to the story, the earth was wandering out of its normal course and growing constantly closer to the sun. As people in the movie conversed, some said they were leaving soon for the north, while others wondered if it was worth the effort. Soon the North Pole, too, would be too hot to survive.

After agonizing scenes of thirsty, frying people throughout almost the entire length of the program, the girl who had been the central figure awoke from sleep and saw that it was snowing outside. All of this terror had been a dream. She exclaimed to the doctor who attended her, "How wonderful it is to see the snow! It feels so good to be cold!" After the doctor moved from her bedside, he asked another member of the family if she was planning to move south to escape the growing cold. Actually, what was happening was that the earth was moving *away* from the sun!

Although I saw that episode nearly fifteen years ago, it is indelibly planted in my mind. As a child, I learned from it great gratitude for the fact that God sits enthroned above the vault of the earth. I knew with deep thanks that He is the One Who keeps the planet in its place and allows the sun's distance to be just right so that earth can survive.

That's the kind of mighty God we have. In stark contrast, we must appear to Him as much less than grasshoppers. *Today's English Version* says, "The people below look as tiny as ants." Even atoms are not small enough to describe our insignificance compared to the One Who sits enthroned above the vault of the earth. Once again the contrast is awe-inspiring. It is a contrast that Isaiah has noted throughout his prophecy, especially in chapter 6, wherein the majesty of God's enthronement could lead only to his remorse. He cried in his despair, "Woe is me... for I am a man of unclean lips." Always the majesty of God reduces us to nothing. His holiness and purity accentuate our sinfulness and filth.

The second set of parallel lines presents a lovely picture of God's stretching out the heavens as a curtain or a tent. After recently moving into a newly built house, I enjoyed fixing up curtains and hanging them, wanting to make them as lovely as possible and choosing bright colors to offset our dreary, gray western Washington skies. It is astounding to try to imagine the vast dimensions of the curtains God hangs. We measure in thousands of miles the firmament that God hangs as easily as we suspend a curtain on a rod. He chooses magnificent colors for His curtains, and even changes them many times each day.

The parallel picture suggests His spreading the heavens like a tent to dwell in. I especially appreciate that picture because it anticipates His future dwelling among us and describes His presence among us now.

The word *tent* and the concept of dwelling are important throughout both the Old and New Testaments. A thread throughout the history of God's people is the concept of God "tabernacling" Himself among us. It begins in the book of Exodus, when God gives specific instructions for His people to construct the tabernacle in which He will dwell. After several chapters of instructions, there are several more chapters in which the construction is completed. Finally, in chapter 40, the most glorious event occurs. God comes to dwell in that tabernacle, and as His overwhelming glory descends upon the tent, the people rejoice. God has surely come and filled the tabernacle with His radiating presence. He fills it so completely that no one can even enter. Glory pulsates from the tent of His presence.

The terrible tragedy of the book of Ezekiel is that this presence departs (although it returns again at the end of the book). Slowly, majestically, the glory of the LORD rises and moves out from the holy place. Hope seems to be crushed forever when it departs from the city of Jerusalem.

The image of dwelling is then picked up again in the gospel of John, when the beloved evangelist writes that the Word became flesh and "tabernacled" Himself among us (1:14). He actually pitched His tent among men to dwell with them for more than thirty years.

Next, in 2 Corinthians 12:9 Paul chooses the same verb to proclaim why he can glory in his suffering. He has talked about his thorn in the flesh and about the grace of God that is sufficient for him. Then he declares, literally, "I shall all the more glory in my weaknesses that the power of God may tabernacle in me." When God tabernacles Himself in us, His grace is all we need. And the point at which He can tabernacle most easily is when we recognize our weakness and invite Him in to dwell. Then His power upon us to conform us to His image can be brought to its finish.

Again, in the book of Revelation, the concept of tabernacling occurs. God declares that He, the Alpha and the Omega, the Beginning and the End, will make His dwelling with men. Both noun and verb forms of tabernacling are used in the twenty-first chapter. Some day He will again "pitch His tent" among men, for He is our God, and we are His people.

Right now, however, the LORD has spread the heavens to be His dwelling tent, as Isaiah declares in verse 22. He wants to tabernacle more thoroughly in our lives.

Together, the two sets of parallel phrases in this verse present the delightful contrast of God's transcendent majesty and His immanent graciousness. God is not only a great God Who accomplishes mighty things, but also a close God Who dwells in our hearts. Even though we are as grasshoppers in comparison to His enthronement upon the vault of the earth, God deigns to spread the heavens like a tabernacle to dwell with us. Some day, we shall hear a voice declare, "Behold, the dwelling of God is with men!"

QUESTIONS FOR FURTHER MEDITATION:

1. With what other pictures can I describe God's enthronement?
2. What other scientific facts, besides the proper distance between the earth and the sun, accentuate the need for God's sovereign care over the vault of the earth?
3. What is the value of recognizing my "grasshopperishness"?
4. What feeling is conveyed to me by the figure of God's stretching out the heavens like a curtain?
5. What other places in the Scriptures emphasize the concept of God's dwelling with His people?
6. How can I experience God's tabernacling in my own heart more thoroughly?
7. What is the value of stressing the future time when God will personally tabernacle among men?

The Cry of Lordship 23

"[It is he] who brings princes to nought,
and makes the rulers of the earth as nothing."
Isaiah 40:23

Only in the fairy tales do princes live happily ever after. In reality, all the princes and rulers of this world have problems of some sort. Some get deposed, some don't get re-elected, and some can't persuade the legislature to go along with their plans. Every ruler has at least a few enemies. None can satisfy every demand.

In fact, Isaiah adds, in relationship to the LORD, the world's rulers are nothing. Literally, the Hebrew phrase describes God as the one "giving the princes to not," and the word for "not" is the same one we encountered in verses 16 and 17. In other words, the princes have no value compared to the reign of Yahweh.

That God reduces the world's princes to nothing is understood by a sort of joke in the Hebrew. The word we translate as "princes" or "rulers" comes from a verb root meaning "to be weighty" or "to be commanding." Thus, the joke is that those who think they have weight, or importance, the LORD brings to "not." Even as the nations are "not" in verse 17, so the LORD reduces the weighty ones to the absence of weight.

The poetic parallel utilizes another striking word that we have encountered previously. The line "and judges of the earth as emptiness He makes" stresses again the meaninglessness of being "without form" that we observed in verse 17 and in Genesis 1:2. The same vacuum that characterized the nations and the world before creation is now shown also to be the truth about the world's rulers.

This verse moves us from the dwellers of the earth in general in

129

the previous verse to its leaders in particular. Prestige and fame, influence and glory are declared to be meaningless. The LORD is the One Who brings to naught those who think they are great, those who assert power in the world.

In Isaiah's time, these comments had a double significance. They spoke to many of the rulers of Israel who were unduly proud and confident of their own power. Also, this verse spoke about the rulers of the nations that threatened Israel. They might appear to have power, but they, too, were nothing in the LORD's hands. He allowed them to chastise His people, but even the great Cyrus fulfilled God's prophecies, made many years before, in allowing the remnant to return from the Babylonian captivity.

As we apply this verse to the contemporary situation, we recognize that the LORD and His justice will ultimately prevail. The message has international, national, and personal consequences.

One way this verse gives us hope internationally is that it helps us realize that we need not fear those rulers who proclaim their greatness in opposition to Christianity. There have been occasions when communist leaders have vowed that they would wipe out the free world and bring it to nothing. We don't have to fear statements like that, because we believe God is sovereign. He is in control, and He will not allow His people to be totally defeated. It is interesting, for example, to observe that Khrushchev, the Russian leader who beat his shoe on the table and vowed U.S. annihilation, was later quietly removed from power and dropped from the memory of the Soviet world.

The Children of Israel provide us with an example of God's fulfillment of His promises to care. Isaiah knew well God's covenant with the chosen people. Although they were a nation of little account, and although they were conquered by mighty nations and taken into captivity, yet a remnant did return. Those mighty nations themselves have long since been destroyed and cut down from their positions of power, whereas the nation of Israel continues to grow.

Nationally, this verse carries a painful reminder and a warning, especially at the time of this writing. When I consider the events in American politics over the last several years, I am struck by the way in which those who sought for power with deceptive and immoral means have been brought to nothing by Watergate and subsequent developments. This verse warns our present leaders to remember their proper place, to realize constantly that the power of earthly authority is vanity.

Most important, however, if we are going to apply this verse honestly to our own lives, we have to realize that it says something to ourselves as individuals. It speaks directly to all our attempts to justify our own existence. It speaks to our need for fame or accomplishment or popularity. It speaks to our desire to assert power over people. It speaks, in summary, to the whole question of the lordship of our lives.

If God is really going to be LORD in our lives, we *CAN'T* be. If Jesus is really King, we cannot be antagonistic princes or princesses, trying to usurp the throne.

One of the songs we sing frequently at our Bible study gatherings addresses this emphasis well. The chorus repeats, "Reign, Lord; O, reign, Lord; reign, Master Jesus, reign. Reign Your Spirit in my heart; Reign, Master Jesus, reign!" Each time we sing that song, I am forced to ask myself if I am really serious about it. Do I really want the LORD to reign in my life, for Jesus to be master over everything?

Unfortunately, far too often you and I are not ready to let the LORD reign. There are times when we choose to go our own directions, to be masters of our own lives, to rule over others so that we can get our own way.

The great discovery of Martin Luther that he recorded in his treatise "Advice to the German Nobility" was that a Christian is a slave of none and master of all; and yet, paradoxically, he is slave to all and master of none. In other words, the Christian is so free from the rule of others that he can willingly submit to them. He is not governed by them, but, therefore, can choose to serve them.

If we thoroughly learn that the LORD brings princes to naught, we will be more willing to forego our attempts to assert power over others. Instead, we will want to ask Him to reign in our lives, wherever that might take us, whatever that might cause us to do, however that might lead us to suffering.

If we want to make that kind of commitment, we have to be serious. It means we will willingly serve no matter the cost. It means we will give up our rights.

I think about this often, particularly in connection with the women's liberation movement. I agree with many of the movement's goals; I especially think women should be allowed to use their gifts responsibly for the benefit of society. Being a woman in a profession formerly reserved for men and enjoying deep friendships with male colleagues who greatly encourage and support my professional growth, I appear to be quite a liberated woman myself. But I disagree strenuously with the basic philosophy underlying the movement. It seems to be founded upon a demand for one's rights.

We cannot clamor for our rights if we really want to follow the LORD's instruction to be the servants of all. If we really want the LORD to be the master in our lives, we must "have this mind among [ourselves], which is yours in Christ Jesus, who, though he was in the form of God, did not count equality with God a thing to be grasped, but emptied Himself, taking the form of a servant" (Phil. 2:5-7). It is imperative, if we really face up to this verse, that we acknowledge the need for humility and submission in our Christian lives. Jesus calls us to give up our rights.

After all, when we really consider life seriously, we remember that power withers, and fame, too, shall fade. What really matters in life are the eternal things, and eternal values have nothing to do with earthly accomplishments. This does not mean that we accept mediocrity or are nonentities. Rather, our desire to be servants causes us to strive after excellence, to serve with the best of our abilities. But our value comes from the importance of our LORD and the fact that He considers us significant. We are not worthless in His gracious sight.

On the other hand, it does mean that we do not strive after fame and power. We all have burning needs to prove ourselves, to show the world that we are valuable. But if we are willing to let God be LORD, He creates our worth and value — eternally. Then our importance will not fade with the passing of time. We will grow more and more willing for God to bring our power to naught so that He might be glorified through us.

This spirit was so beautifully demonstrated by John the Baptizer when he was questioned about the fact that Jesus was baptizing more than he. John replied, "He must increase, but I must decrease" (John 3:30). If Isaiah's words are seriously confronted in our lives, that must also be our response. The more we want to live to the glory of God, the more we will desire His presence in our lives to increase and our selfish egos to decrease.

That is not to say that we won't be fulfilled in our lives. In fact, the paradoxical truth is that we will be far more deeply satisfied. We will be otherwise directed; we will seek not after our own needs but after the needs of others. Devoting our lives to greater ends than our own happinesses by meeting the needs of those around us, we will discover that true happiness is a by-product, not to be found when we are looking for it but to be received as a gift when we give ourselves totally to the Creator of all Joy.

It is so exciting that the LORD brings our attempts at importance to naught. Then He can confer upon us the greatest significance of all, His rule in our lives.

QUESTIONS FOR FURTHER MEDITATION:

1. How have I seen in history that princes are brought to naught?
2. How have I seen that power in the world's sense is meaningless?
3. What should be the attitude of Christians in positions of leadership?
4. How can I assist Christian leaders in recognizing the truth of this verse and its application to their lives?
5. How can I strive after excellence without elevating my ego?
6. What does it mean to be a servant after the pattern of Christ?
7. How can I grow in my spirit of servanthood?

The Cry of Temporality 24

"Scarcely are they planted, scarcely sown,
scarcely has their stem taken root in the earth,
when he blows upon them, and they wither,
and the tempest carries them off like stubble."

Isaiah 40:24

There's a huge difference between the way I plant things and the way my grandfather does. Three words summarize all the contrasts between his garden and mine: his grows well! When I was a child, Grandfather grew all sorts of things and was often praised for having such outstanding crops. He supplied all the neighbors with plenty of vegetables for the winter. He took care of all the flowers in the yard and had all sorts of violets and trailing vines throughout his house. I don't try to keep many plants in my home; I know too well what would happen if I did. Flowers I was given once, back when I was an English teacher, toppled over a few weeks after they germinated. Scarcely had they taken root when they withered away.

That is the way Isaiah describes the princes of the earth. He uses a negative particle at the beginning of each of the first three phrases in verse 24 to express an action hardly even commenced. "Yea, scarcely shall they be planted, scarcely shall they be sown, scarcely rooted in the earth their stalk — until he shall blow upon them." The last of these three events is in a participial form, which connects it more closely to the following comment and which seems to imply that the plants' taking root might not even quite have happened.

Then, when the LORD blows upon them, "They shall dry up." Both of these verbs about the blowing and the drying up are repetitions of the word choices in verses 7 and 8. Consequently, they bring to our minds the comments there about all flesh being grass. This time, however, Isaiah adds that "the whirlwind as

135

stubble shall lift them up." The verb used in this last phrase is
also a repetition of one used earlier. In both verses 4 and 11, this
word is used in a positive sense to speak of the exalting of the
valleys and of the shepherd's carrying of the lambs. Here,
negatively, the world's rulers are lifted up by the storms as easily
as if they were straw.

This verse adds several significant dimensions to the emphasis
on impermanence from previous verses (especially vv. 6-8). Particular stress seems to be placed on the contrast between the
impermanence of the planting and the finality of the carrying
away. Scarcely have they taken root when the breath of the LORD
dries them up and the whirlwind carries them away. Those who
rest in their own power might think they are firmly rooted, but
the LORD's blowing upon them proves them wrong. The power of
flesh can not be firmly rooted. The whirlwinds and the LORD's
blowing just accentuate the inherent problem that the plants are
not thriving, but are only stubble.

In contrast, those who depend on the power of God and not
their flesh can be firmly planted. Many images of the New Testament speak of our being rooted and grounded. For example, in
Ephesians 3, after Paul says, "I bow my knees before the Father,
from whom every family in heaven and on earth is named," he
prays for the Ephesian people, that they might become so rooted
and grounded in Christ's love that they might know its length and
breadth and depth and height (vv. 17-18).

Similarly, in Colossians 2, Paul prays that just as the people
trusted Christ for salvation, so they might also trust Him for each
day's problems; that rooted and grounded in Him, they might
grow up to know the fullness of His provision for their needs. (vv.
6-7). Paul's prayers help us realize that there is no way to avoid
being blown away other than to be rooted in Christ.

We might carry the comparison of my grandfather's plants to
mine a bit further here. One of the reasons his plants do so much
better is that he continues to care for them diligently. He follows
up on the planting and spends time making sure that everything
is conducive to the plants' best growth. Just so, the rooting and
grounding of which Paul speaks depend on careful nurturing.

Perhaps Jesus was thinking of this verse from Isaiah when He told His parable of the sower (Matt. 13). Those seeds that fell among the stones sprang up without depth and, consequently, were scorched and withered away (vv. 5-6). What is suggested is the superficiality of it all. What a contrast God's values are to the values of man! We think prestige is of great value; we think our power is a mighty thing. Isaiah's words remind us that the LORD brings the world's leadership to naught, simply by blowing upon it.

Perhaps Isaiah's last phrase, that the whirlwind carries them away like stubble, is analogous to both the seed planted in the path and that which fell among thorns (Matt. 13:4, 7). Either we are carried away by Satan or choked out by the cares of the world. Both have the effect of a whirlwind on strawlike faith.

The conclusion of Jesus' parable gives us the positive hope for this verse from Isaiah. Rather than be carried away or dried up because we have not been adequately planted, we must make sure that the seed — the Word of God, Jesus says — falls on good soil and bears fruit (Matt. 13:8). We must be rooted and grounded in Christ, as Paul wrote to the Philippians and Colossians.

The Living Bible's paraphrase gives additional insight with these words: "They hardly get started, barely take root, when he blows on them and their work withers and the wind carries them off like straw." The addition of the word *work* gives us a particular dimension of life to consider. When the princes are brought to naught, their works will be revealed for their true value. This image, too, is reinforced in the New Testament when Paul speaks about works being tested by fire so that it might be shown what a man is and what he has done (1 Cor. 3:12-13). When our works are tested by the LORD's blowing, if they are impermanent works of stubble, they wither and are carried away.

This is a critical point for consideration when we decide how to spend our time. Are we spending our time to do things that wither when the LORD blows upon them, things that are mere straw and should be carried away, things that indicate our lack of depth? Rather, we can choose to do things with our time that will have permanent value, things that will be tested by fire and revealed for the truly eternal things they are.

We need to understand this perspective in order to catch sight of what genuinely gives life value and meaning. When we seek for power or for our own gain, when we choose to make ourselves princes, we find that we have no lasting authority. Our work will be carried away because we ourselves are stubble. Instead, we can choose to be servants, desiring to elevate Christ. When our goal is for Him to be glorified, when we make ourselves of no reputation as He did and choose to be involved in eternal things, our work will have lasting value.

What are those eternal things that are called works of gold in 1 Corinthians 3? Every time I stop to think about this, I am overwhelmed with the realization that the only thing that really matters is the saving of souls. If all of us are only grass, our time should be spent proclaiming only that which stands forever. Is my whole life invested in sharing the gospel? Is yours?

One of the major failures of many contemporary churches is that we have lost sight of the fact that our whole lifestyle as Christians is to be evangelistic. Scarcely is anything else planted that the LORD's breath does not cause to wither, and the whirl-winds blow it away. Isaiah's words are a challenge to us to realize that the only work we can do that can have important conse-quences (those that will last forever) is to be involved in people's lives, caring for their spiritual welfare and helping them to be rooted and grounded eternally.

QUESTIONS FOR FURTHER MEDITATION:
1. In what things do I try in vain to develop roots?
2. How do I become more securely rooted in Christ?
3. What works have I done that seemed mighty and lasting, but were shown to be merely stubble?
4. What kinds of things dry me up?
5. What will cause the difference between difficulties drying me up and the same trials causing me to dig my roots down more deeply to get at the moisture I need?
6. What kinds of whirlwinds blow me away?
7. What can my church be doing to help Christians get rooted more thoroughly?

The Cry of Holiness 25

"To whom then will you compare me,
that I should be like him? says the Holy One."
Isaiah 40:25

Consider Bjorn Borg. As I write this, he has just won his third straight Wimbledon tennis championship. This is the first time someone has done that for more than forty years. Suppose he said to us, "Now, to whom will you compare me, that I could be as good as he?"

"Borg *as good as* someone else?" we would exclaim. "Why, he's so much better than all the rest!" What a foolish question!

That is the irony of the LORD's question in verse 25. "To whom will you liken me," the Holy One says, "to be comparable?" Of course, the phrase implies that He is incomparable. What could be set up to be of like value to the LORD? According to Hebrew law, if I killed your ox, I would have to give you a sum of money equal to its value. Similarly, the Holy One seems to ask, "What could you put up, that I should match the funds?"

The question is so backward it's ludicrous. Anyone that man could propose to compare is so feeble in relation to the LORD that it would take Him no time to prove Himself infinitely more than a mere countervailing equal. Indeed, God is equal to far more than everything and everyone put all together all at once.

For the first time in this fortieth chapter, the LORD calls Himself the Holy One, a name for Him frequently used elsewhere in the book of Isaiah. The term, *kadosh*, means that God is separated, set apart in His purity. Vessels that were *kadosh* were separated for use in the temple because they had been particularly consecrated by the Children of Israel. The LORD, on the other hand, is separated not because man has so designated Him, but because

139

that is His very character. That is why there is no one to whom He can be compared. No one else is so separated.

The irony of the question that God asks heightens the uniqueness of His characterization as the "Holy One." Immediately, there comes to my mind the man with an unclean spirit who, upon meeting Jesus, cried out, "What have you to do with us, Jesus of Nazareth?... I know who you are, the Holy One of God" (Mark 1:24). His shuddering terror underscores the fact that evil cannot tolerate the vision of holiness. As he confronted Him, the unclean spirit could not stand before the holiness of Jesus; the Holy One cast him out.

Evil cannot tolerate a vision of holiness, nor can the Holy One tolerate the presence of evil. Consequently, the name "Holy One," as applied to God, must fill us with abject terror. This is the atmosphere that we observe in the story of the calling of the prophet in Isaiah 6. He sees the Holy One, high and lifted up, with His train filling the temple. The cherubim and seraphim sing antiphonally, calling out, "Holy, holy, holy is the LORD of hosts; the whole earth is full of his glory" (6:3). Immediately Isaiah reacts in fear. He is overwhelmed with grief and cries out, "Woe is me! For I am lost; for I am a man of unclean lips,... for my eyes have seen the King, the LORD of hosts!" (6:5). When we are confronted with the holiness of God, we cannot help but realize the total absence of holiness in our lives, our complete lack of worth before the LORD.

We experience such jarring contrasts often in mere human terms. For example, consider how you feel when someone much wiser, much richer, or much more beautiful sits beside you. You cannot help but compare yourself and realize your inferiority. I always felt so small as a beginning organ student in college when some of the real musicians, who had been playing the organ for years, would come to hear us play our first-year recital pieces. When we multiply that embarrassment an infinite number of times and then add a load of guilt and shame besides, we can begin to discover what it is like to face the holiness of God.

Critical to the background of the Reformation is the fact that Luther was uniquely terrified by the Holy One and filled with trepidation because he did not know how to please Him. He tried everything — doing every conceivable sort of penance, beating his own body mercilessly, confessing the smallest of sins and even some he had not committed — and yet he was utterly aware that he could never please a holy God.

When we put that sense of the LORD's holiness into the context of this verse, we are aghast at man's audacity. What presumption that we should think we could compare anything to God! All creation is the product of His Word. Yet all His works have been adversely affected by man's Fall, and thereby rendered imperfect. We brought all the trouble into this world and marred God's created order. How could we suppose to set up anyone to whom we might compare Him Who is the Holy One?

The holiness of God has many important implications. For example, a character that is perfectly holy must also, of necessity, embody perfect Truth. That means I can confidently trust that my relationship with God is the ultimate reality. Always I can trust that God will be totally faithful to His character. I can know that He will always be the same yesterday, today, and forever in eternity (Heb. 13:8). His holiness implies consistency. Perfection means constancy.

For that reason, as Luther discovered (and found himself set free by it), we can come boldly into the presence of the Holy One, knowing that the constancy of His grace and the perfection of His love caused Him to send His Son to secure holiness for us. The Holy One's attitude toward us is characterized fundamentally by grace, and that grace is applied to us to make us holy.

Consequently, our Joy as Christians is the realization that God has called us to be holy unto Him. He has said, "You shall be holy to me; for I the LORD am holy, and have separated you from the peoples, that you should be mine" (Lev. 20:26; see also 1 Pet. 1:16). We do not become holy unto Him because of our efforts at holiness. We become holy because He is holy, and He has set us apart. As Isaiah confessed his unholiness in chapter 6, the angel flew to him with tongs holding a burning coal. Cleansing was completed, and Isaiah was sent out to be the messenger of the LORD. His grief over his uncleanness was transformed into eagerness to serve.

The process is the same for us. The apostle John tells us in his first epistle, "If we confess our sins, he is faithful and just, and will forgive our sins and cleanse us from all unrighteousness" (1:9). That the LORD provided for our cleansing is part of His character as the Holy One. In His holiness, He desires fellowship with a holy people. He has planned for His people to be set apart unto Him, to be separated from the world so that we can be His.

How can we compare the LORD to anything else? Could there ever be anyone like Him? It seems we wouldn't need to ask those questions again, for we have confronted them seriously in previous verses. But we must ask them again in light of God's holiness.

We must realize anew each day that the LORD alone is holy. That is a shattering discovery. We couldn't survive it if we didn't also know the perfection of His grace.

QUESTIONS FOR FURTHER MEDITATION:
1. How is the holiness of God revealed?
2. How should I define the word *holy*?
3. How does the holiness of God present to me both the Law and the gospel?
4. What does it mean that I am called to be holy?
5. Is it possible for me to strive after holiness?
6. How can I avoid the extremes of thinking I can earn holiness and despairing because I can't?
7. How will my holiness reveal itself?

The Cry of Significance 26

"Lift up your eyes on high and see:
who created these?
He who brings out their host by number,
calling them all by name;
by the greatness of his might,
and because he is strong in power
not one is missing."

Isaiah 40:26

I lay awake half the night, gazing at the stars. It was an incredible display. All the girls from our choir and all the women students at the Christian Medical College in Vellore, India, were sleeping out on the roof of the girls' dorm. It hadn't rained for years, and the sky was crystal clear. I had never known there were so many stars. I was awestruck by the majesty of God visible in their splendor. Each time I closed my eyes, I had to open them right up again to make sure they were all still there.

We can't be certain that Isaiah is speaking about the stars, because the word for them does not occur in the original Hebrew of this verse, but his comments seem to suggest them. "Lift up on high your eyes and see," he commands. The first verb is an imperative form of the same verb we discussed in verses 4, 11, and 24. Now the prophet's listeners are urged to take a specific action to observe more carefully. When they have done so, they will be forced by what they have seen to ask, "Who created these?" The standard demonstrative pronoun translated "these" could refer to anything observable on high. But stars do seem to be the most likely subject.

The description of the Creator of these heavenly objects begins with a participial construction that says literally, "The bringer-out by number of their host." Unless otherwise specified (as in the phrase, "the hosts of Israel"), this last term is associated with the heavenly hosts, as in the most common expression, "The LORD of hosts." All the armies of angels, all the beings of the heavens, are suggested.

The One bringing them out does so by number. The singular form of this term suggests individuality. He brings them out personally, one by one, as if to count them off.

That individual attention is accentuated by the next phrase, "to all of them by name He calls." Because of our New Testament understanding of Jesus as the Good Shepherd, this line has a special significance for us. Jesus asserts in John 10 that the Good Shepherd knows His sheep. He calls them by name and leads them out (v. 3). Here the Creator, Who was also called a Shepherd in verse 11, is pictured with the same tenderness, calling out all the hosts of heaven individually, by name. The imperfect form of the verb suggests not the original naming of those beings (a completed action), but a continual calling (incompleted action) by their individual names.

Furthermore, because of "the great might and powerful strength" of the "Bringer," not one is missing. The four terms used to describe His omnipotence will be more significant when we study verse 29, where they are used again and reveal a progression in thought. At this point only the first of the four is a term of quantity, meaning "much" or "many." The other three terms suggest almightiness.

Because of their Bringer's power, not one of the host is missing. The Hebrew sentence actually says, "A man is not missing." Such anthropomorphism accentuates the verse's individualizing. Since in this verse Isaiah has also used the term *hosts*, which suggests military forces, the Hebrew professor with whom I was studying this text quipped, "Not even a private is out of the ranks." The picture is a graphic image of the "great might and powerful strength" of Yahweh. Not one of all the myriads of angels, stars, or whatever that He has created will ever fail or cease without His plan. He is able both to call each one forth by name and to hold each one in its perfectly appointed place.

This verse is stupendously comforting. The prophet calls us to look to the hosts of the heavens and recognize by our vision their testimony to the power and greatness of the LORD.

The stars have always been an impressive thing to man, so impressive that he has tried to chart his future by them. God used a special star to enable the Magi to find the Messiah. We thought of that the night we sang a concert in Bethlehem, and the sky was ablaze with stars. Although it was July 19, they were so brilliant and lovely that we were all sure it was Christmas — the first Christmas — and we sang Christmas carols on the bus all the way back to Jerusalem.

Lift up your eyes on high and see: Who created these? Is there any doubt?

We cannot help but be awed by the tremendous plan of God when we look at the vast array of stars. Yet they each have their assigned place. I am sure that it is even more meaningful to us now than it was in Isaiah's time, because we know that those places aren't all stationary. God charted all the patterns of the movements of all the planets and galaxies so that they wouldn't collide. Our modern telescopes search beyond galaxies beyond other galaxies, and yet they cannot comprehend the infinity of stardom.

Furthermore, for God to call each one of the host by name means that they aren't just a vast array of meaningless bright fires or reflections. Each has a name. That implies a distinctive character, a quality all its own. As we think of God's calling the heavenly hosts out by name, we realize that He has called out each dimension of His creation personally. He has assigned to each particular creature or body its nature, its function, its characteristics, its uniqueness. God has been very specific in His creation.

Similarly, He has been very specific in His creation of each of us. As we ponder the multitudes of planets and stars, we naturally think about the many people who inhabit the earth. Yet each one is distinct. Each one has his very own name, a character by which he is known. You and I are each unique. God created us that way, and He calls us by name to deal with us personally and to accentuate our individuality. In Isaiah 43:1, the LORD says, "I have called you by name, you are mine."

Finally, we are reminded by the prophet that God's plan is so perfect and His omnipotence so complete that never is anything missing. Jesus says, "Consider the lilies... and the birds of the air." Here we realize that even all the falling stars are counted when they fall. Even the very hairs of our heads are numbered.

The application to our lives is significant. If God takes that kind of care for stars and lilies and birds, how much more deeply does He care for souls? Not only does He invest each person with a particular name and character, but also He is sure that never is anyone missing. By His pure grace and great power, surely each one is particularly and personally cared for.

The psalmist promises us, "No good thing does the LORD withhold from those who walk uprightly" (84:11). When God promises that not a man is missing, it helps us to realize that none of the many blessings God could pour out upon us will be missing either (see the following chapter). Not one that is necessary for our well-being will we ever have to do without. The LORD always provides sufficiently. None of the angel hosts who carry out His purposes are ever missing from His service.

QUESTIONS FOR FURTHER MEDITATION:

1. What besides the stars in a vast array gives me insight into beauty as God created it?

2. How is the contrast of the vast array and yet God's individual attention to each member of the vast array revealed to me?

3. How do I recognize God's infinite use of His power and might on my behalf?

4. What do I do with the feelings that I have sometimes that something I need is missing, that God has not sufficiently provided for all my needs?

5. How do I know that each one of us is important to God?

6. How does the fact that not one is missing relate to the doctrine of eternal security?

7. What can my church do to help each person know that he or she is important?

The Cry against Complaining 27

"Why do you say, O Jacob,
and speak, O Israel,
'My way is hid from the LORD
and my right is disregarded by my God'?"
Isaiah 40:27

Mother caught us swiping cookies. My brother and
I thought we could get away without her seeing us. Sometimes it
seemed that she had eyes in the back of her head. Our way could
not be hidden from her.

Isaiah criticizes collectively the Children of Israel for thinking
that their way was hidden from Yahweh. The word translated
"way" in our versions means one's "lifestyle," or "daily conduct."
The verb is in a perfect form, which implies a completed action —
not that Israel's patterns of behavior are in the process of being
hidden, but that the way is already hidden. Together these word
choices suggest that Jacob thinks his course of conduct can
escape or has escaped God's notice.

The poetic parallel says literally, "and from *Elohim* my judgment is passed over." This same word for judgment occurred
previously in verse 14 and might imply either a negative sentence
or a positive justice. The verb "to pass over" is the one used to
speak of fording a river to get beyond it. It might suggest that the
sentence Jacob should be under is not being executed.

Together these two lines could be interpreted either in the
sense of Jacobean deceptiveness or in the sense of the typical
Israelite complaining. In the first sense, the Children of Israel
would be exulting, "God doesn't see our misbehavior. We don't
have to worry because we can escape the sentence we deserve."
In the second sense, they would be mourning, "God just doesn't
see our lot; our rights are being disregarded by our God."

Both interpretations fit in with Isaiah's pointed questions, "Why

147

do you say [this], O Jacob, and speak [in this way], O Israel?"
Both cunning and complaint have no place among the people of
God. Both interpretations offer us significant lessons concerning
our attitudes about God's place and action in our lives.

We must recognize, first of all, that Isaiah's admonition is necessary. Why do the Israelites speak as they do? What gives them
cause to complain or to seek to deceive God and get away with
apathy or disobedience? Isaiah reminds the people, and us, that it
is impossible for one's way to be hidden from the LORD, much as
they, and we in the twentieth century, might like to try. Our road
cannot be hidden from One Who doesn't even let one of the stars
be missing. On the basis of the evidence from the last verse, why
do we say, as Jacob, that God doesn't observe our behavior? Why
do we think, as Israel, that our rights are being disregarded by
our God? Surely we need the rhetorical questions of the next
verse to remind us that we ought to pay better attention to what
we have known and heard.

It was appalling to me to recognize, as I pondered this verse,
how often I assume both the attitudes suggested by these questions. Times when I think I'm getting away with things, I don't
stop to realize how cognizant the LORD is of everything I do and
how precisely He understands all my feelings, motives, and
thoughts.

It is impossible to hide from the LORD, and yet how often we
try. We think we can escape His sentence and the judgment we
deserve. We think we can get into the cookies without being
noticed.

But our sin will find us out. We cannot get away with it. When
we lie, we have to tell other lies to cover up the first one. When
we deceive others, we lose their trust and spoil our relationships.
When we act contrary to our Christian principles, our consciences
plague us and even cause us to suffer physically. Ultimately, sin
always produces its own destructive consequences. We can't escape
the judgment we deserve.

On the other hand, the second interpretation of this text con-
fronts us with our blind folly at those times when we judge God.
We shout that He is not acting toward us as we deserve. We
demand that we get justice, and we cry to secure our rights.

Contrarily, the apostle Paul offers us the model of Christ Jesus, Who, although He was God, did not demand His rights as God (Phil. 2:5-11). He genuinely deserved them, but He didn't demand them. We don't deserve them, but we insist that we get them. When we honestly consider our character as the self-centered people we are (apart from the grace of God), we realize that truly we do not deserve any rights in the first place.

The *Today's English Version* rendering of this verse adds a special emphasis when it says, "Israel, why then do you complain that the LORD doesn't know your troubles or care if you suffer injustice?" Similarly, *The Living Bible* suggests: "O Jacob, O Israel, how can you say that the Lord doesn't see your troubles and isn't being fair?" Those words summarize the problem underlying much of our complaining. If we gripe about the particulars of our situations, we are expressing the attitude that the Lord doesn't know our troubles, that He doesn't care if we suffer injustice, that He isn't being fair.

What folly for us to feel that way! Yet merely to tell ourselves we are wrong does not change the feelings. We need, instead, to face up to what those feelings are really saying, both about ourselves and about our God. When we've become convinced that God must not know our situation very well or He wouldn't deal with us so unjustly, we are forgetting that our way cannot be hidden from the LORD. He does not disregard our rights, but, rather, He knows what would be the very best for us. We need to learn to know Him better in order to trust more thoroughly His plan for our lives.

His plan might entail the supposed infringement of some of our rights, and yet the LORD never denies us the right of being His children (John 1:12). He never withholds from us the rights of salvation or eternal life — not earned or deserved by us, but bestowed upon us by His grace. "Blessed," Jesus calls us when we go without our rights for the sake of the Kingdom of God (Matt. 5:3-11). The rights for which we fight and manipulate others as human beings are oftentimes mirages, not really rights at all, and certainly not satisfying. The LORD Who is sovereign over all the heavenly hosts calls them out by name so that not one is missing. Certainly He is just as particular about our rights. On the basis of the picture of God in verse 26, Isaiah asks the question of this verse, in anticipation of the rebuke in verse 28.

Isaiah's indictment in this verse teaches an important lesson about complaining. We can so easily get caught up in a bitter and complaining spirit that we don't realize what our murmuring and discontent say about the LORD. To complain is to accuse Him of not being aware of what is going on. To grumble about our situation suggests that we think our way is hidden from His wise planning.

A lovely plaque that I have seen in several Christian bookstores asserts, "The Lord gives the best to those who leave the choice with Him." Whenever we complain and want things to go our way, we are believing that our sense of justice is better than God's. It is indeed idolatry when we thereby place our own intelligence above the wisdom of the LORD. When we value our own wisdom and reason above His, we violate the first commandment, which is to love God with our whole heart and soul and *mind*.

Perhaps you share my perennial problem with complaining. It is so easy for me to fall into bad habits of mistrust. If things don't go right, I'm immediately upset. On the contrary, the substance of a sure and mature faith is that the person knows his way is fully perceived by God, and dealt with accordingly. Consequently, the believer trusts that all things do indeed work together for good to them that love God (Rom. 8:28).

My lack of faith is terribly obvious. Even as I work today, I'm afraid I won't be able to get everything done that I "need" to do. It seems that I'm thinking my way is hidden from God, or that this is something He's just not able to handle. I am ashamed as I read this verse. I am ashamed of my negative spirit. I'm ashamed of my failure to comprehend that God does indeed want to work through me all the things that really "need" to be done. I am ashamed that I do not realize that God alone is just and right, and that all things that flow from Him must, necessarily, be so also. But I am thankful that God doesn't deal with me according to my shame.

QUESTIONS FOR FURTHER MEDITATION:

1. How can I realize more thoroughly that I can't get away with sin?

2. Does the fact that Christians many times have to suffer injustice make this verse a lie?

3. If God knows my way, why doesn't He act to change things in me that are bad?

4. How can I avoid a complaining and contentious spirit?

5. How can I learn better that my rights are given to me by God according to my needs?

6. How can I learn voluntarily to give up my rights?

7. How should my church best deal with questions of personal rights?

The Cry of Everlastingness 28

"Have you not known? Have you not heard?
The LORD is the everlasting God,
the Creator of the ends of the earth.
He does not faint or grow weary,
his understanding is unsearchable."
Isaiah 40:28

Do you remember the time when you first discovered the idea of infinity? What a mind-boggling experience! I can hear myself asking, "You mean there is no beginning and no end?" Uh huh. "It goes on and on and on and never stops?" Uh huh. "But it's got to stop somewhere!" Huh uh. "It really is everlasting?" Uh huh. And so I discovered something new about God, and I caught my first glimpse of the idea that my own new existence in heaven would also be eternal. What an exciting, impossible prospect, an incredible possiblity!

Somehow we lose our excitement about the everlastingness of God. That is what seems to have happened to the Children of Israel. Consequently, everlastingness is the theme of this verse. Its tones ring out not only in the words and phrases themselves, but also in the Hebrew constructions and the progression of thought from previous verses.

The verse begins with the same idea as the opening of verse 21, but with two noteworthy changes. First, in verse 21, the phrases "Do you not know? Are you not hearing?" utilize a second person plural verb, whereas here the form is singular in keeping with verse 27, in which the people were addressed collectively, as one — as Jacob and as Israel.

Second, the verb construction has changed from an imperfect form, which signifies incompleted action, to a perfect form, which means a completed action. In verse 21 the people are asked, "Are you still not knowing?" and "will you not hear?" Here the questions have become, "Have you not known? Have you not heard?"

153

After the prophet's criticism of their complaining, he almost seems to be saying, "This is your last chance, Israel. You ought to have understood by now." And so he ushers in the final argument, which will be developed in four verses, dealing with the concept of becoming faint, or growing weary.

Immediately after the indicting questions, God is defined by His relationship to everlastingness. The Hebrew form of the words actually means, "God of everlastingness." This is the God Who is Yahweh, the covenant LORD of the Children of Israel. Then follow three pictures that enable us to observe how His everlastingness can be recognized.

First, He is "the Creator of the ends of the earth." This means not only that He created all the earth and everything in it, but also that He created its boundaries. Even though we think it is terrifically large, the earth has its limits, its "farthest parts" (TLB). God, on the other hand, has no beginning and no end.

Second, "He does not become faint or grow weary." As we shall see in later verses, others do become tired. Here the verb is in an imperfect form of continuous action. God continues not to become faint or weak. Instead, He continues to work without ever getting tired.

Finally, "of His understanding [there is] no searching." The preposition introducing His understanding means "as far as" or "penetration of," and the noun for "understanding" is the same one we met at the end of verse 14. The same root had also occurred in a verb form at the beginning of that verse. The phrase means, then, that as far as His understanding is concerned, there can be no searching of it. The human mind cannot penetrate it.

Isaiah's rhetorical questions respond to the previous complaints by the people about God's lack of justice. The prophet emphasizes that if the people had known and heard (as suggested previously), they wouldn't be speaking as they were. The critical element is what they should have known, namely, the everlastingness of God. The One Who is our covenant God is the God Who alone is everlasting. God's plan from before all of time extends into time and goes right on through time on our behalf. Because He is everlasting, we can trust Him to unfold His plan perfectly.

Part of His plan was effected when He created the ends of the earth. His power and might stretch forever; all things are under His control. By His "great might and powerful strength" (v. 26), nothing is missing. All the way to the ends of the earth, nothing escapes the notice of our God. Surely, our way cannot be hidden from Him Who sees to the ends of the earth.

Furthermore, He does not become faint or grow weary. One of the strongest testimonies to the power of God is that after doing all that He does, He still keeps on following up on His work. Not only did He create the world, but He continues to preserve it. Not only did He save us, but He continues to work in us to conform us to the image of His Son, and to do His work through us. God does not just begin tasks and then leave them half finished. He continues to care and to provide and to sustain.

This is hard to imagine: God is never tired. Even as I revise these words, I must pause occasionally to rest. I need to take naps in the middle of very busy days. Imagine how God works constantly, doing everything all at once all the time, and yet He's not tired tomorrow. Nor does He go to sleep tonight. We can call on Him in the middle of the night. We can call on Him time and time and time again, and all of us at once, and He will remain patient and forbearing, ready to receive and answer our calls. He never grows faint or weary, but is constantly ready to help the oppressed, the needy, the comfortless, the desolate.

Finally, Isaiah adds the phrase, "His understanding is unsearchable." If we cannot figure out why God behaves toward us as He does, we cannot attribute it to His being tired or too weary to help us. Rather, we must recognize that we cannot understand His understanding. This gives an especially specific response to the previous verse and enables us to have hope in our waiting. When we might wish for God to act mightily on our behalf, or when we ask Him to move in quickly to change a situation, we need to understand that it is not because He is not able or does not want to that He does not intervene immediately. He has reasons infinitely beyond our understanding. Many mysteries of God are not yet unfolded.

The fact that His understanding is unsearchable gives a foundation for much of the rest of Isaiah 40. We don't understand why the grass is blown away. We can't understand the problem of pain.

But God understands, and we know that His character is to be just and gracious and righteous. Therefore, we can trust His understanding. We believe that His understanding is right, truly in accordance with genuine reality, even though we cannot comprehend it. Consequently, we are driven to a deeper love for His infinity, a greater gratitude for His provision for our needs. We know God has spent all His energies on us without becoming faint. He has devoted Himself totally to us and to our needs, without growing weary of us.

I grow very weary in devotion. Just yesterday I should have been ministering to the gentleman I was with, but I had a severe headache and so, thinking only of myself, I was terribly crabby. My friend was kind, but I was so tired. Not much ministry came from me. How much more must God, in human terms, get tired of ministering to me when my relationship to Him is fraught with misbehaviors, bad attitudes, and my failures to trust Him! My needs seem so important to me. Scrutinized against an eternal perspective, they are not all that major. Yet I allow myself to get all caught up in them and become filled with tension. Why do I worry about God's provision when I can trust that He does not grow weary of caring? He knows my needs and understands what I am going through.

One of the most precious assurances for our humanity is that Jesus has undergone every temptation and trial to which we are subject, so that He eternally understands (Heb. 4:15). We cannot even begin to comprehend how deeply He understands, because He knows our feelings both from a man's perspective and from God's perspective.

For several months this year I experienced the deepest depression of my life. I had been deceived and torn apart by two of my best friends, and I just couldn't put the pieces of my life back together. One night, engulfed in a black gloom, I screamed at God, "You don't understand! You don't know what it's like to be so bitterly betrayed!" O, Jesus! At last I am just beginning to understand the suffering You bore for me!

This verse makes me want to cry out with Job, "Though he slay me, yet will I trust in him" (Job 13:15, KJV), or with Habakkuk, "Though the fig tree do not blossom, nor fruit be on the vines, . . .

yet I will rejoice in the LORD, I will joy in the God of my salvation. GOD, the Lord, is my strength; he makes my feet like hinds' feet, he makes me tread upon my high places" (Hab. 3:17-19). God's understanding is unsearchable, but I do know that it includes perfect purposes for me. I can trust His high purposes. We can trust that He never becomes faint; especially, He never grows weary in well-doing.

It's time for you and I to know. Pay attention now, and let us hear. For Yahweh is the God of everlastingness.

QUESTIONS FOR FURTHER MEDITATION:

1. What kinds of things are helping me to know and hear better as I grow in my Christian life?

2. What does the concept of everlastingness mean?

3. How does the fact of God's everlastingness affect my relationship with Him in this life?

4. How does modern man indicate by his behavior that he believes God is tired or has limited understanding?

5. How might the situations I encounter be dealt with differently if I have the perspective that the LORD is a God of everlastingness?

6. How does it comfort me to know that God's understanding is unsearchable?

7. How would greater consciousness of God's everlastingness affect my church?

The Cry of Empowering 29

"He gives power to the faint,
and to him who has no might he increases strength."
Isaiah 40:29

Clifford Schultz, one of the mightiest men I have ever known, was almost completely incapacitated by advancing multiple sclerosis. The vibrancy of his faith and witness moved literally hundreds of people. He always had a good word of encouragement for everyone he met, especially the other patients at the convalescent home where he lived. All who visited him were uplifted by his strength. No one could ever doubt Who was the Source and Giver of that immense strength.

Isaiah does a fascinating thing with word choices in this verse to accentuate the strength of that Giver. He makes use of several words from verses 26 and 28 to underscore the relationship and the contrast between God and man. The contrast is further heightened by a change in the proportion of terms of quantity and of power from verse 26. A careful look at all the special word choices multiplies the impact of this verse on our lives.

The verse begins with a participial phrase; that Yahweh is the subject is understood. Isaiah calls Him "The One giving to the faint strength." The word for "faint" is the first of the two qualities denied in the character of God in verse 28, and the word for "strength" is the final term of the four ascribed to God in verse 26. Thus, to those not like Him because they are weak, the LORD imparts a bit of Himself. He confers upon them His strength.

The poetic parallel, "and to the one without might He increases vastness," uses two other terms from verse 26. The word for "might" is the second of the four words that make up the series describing God's omnipotence. There God possesses it; here man is without it. Then the verb translated "increases" in this verse is a verb form of the first term in the verse 26 series. The only term that is not repeated in verse 29 from that series is the third word, which we translated "powerful." In its place is substituted a Hebrew word that sounds very much like it, so perhaps Isaiah intended a play on words. This new term, instead of stressing the idea of power, signifies vastness or multiplication or making more tangible. In other words, on behalf of the one lacking might, Yahweh increases the multiplication of it.

I like to call "stacking" the Hebrew thought pattern that underlies this image. When the Old Testament people used such multiplied terms, they didn't think of them as just being added together, but as multiplied to the second term's power. Instead of three plus three, for example, a repetition of three would really mean three times three times three. Or the phrase "ages upon ages" would not mean just ages plus ages, but ages times ages times ages times ages to the "agesth" power (if that could be a word). We use the same thought pattern when we say something is multiplied to the "nth" degree. Here, then, Isaiah means that God increases might to the multiplied degree, a powerful increase to be sure!

This striking image is reinforced by the progression from verse 26, which can now be specified. There God was described with three terms of power and only one term of quantity. Here in verse 29, what He does for man is asserted with two terms of power and a deliberate (emphasized by a play on words) increase to two terms of quantity. God possesses such a great quantity of power; when He gives it to men, theirs must be multiplied to a double degree.

Even as I write this chapter, I am greatly cheered by this verse and its promise that when we are weary, God multiplies our strength with His. *Today's English Version* calls the recipients of God's strength "those who are weak and tired," and *The Living Bible* says, "He gives power to the tired and worn out." We all experience times when we have no strength left. At those times, what a Joy it is to know that our God of "great might and powerful strength," Who never gets tired Himself, passes on His strength to His people. He gives vigor to us when we are exhausted. In fact, His power flows through us best when we are powerless.

As I have studied church history in my seminary training, I have been astounded at the mighty things God has drawn out of the weakness of His people. The church in general and specific saints in particular, humble people like Francis of Assisi or William Carey, have manifested extraordinary strength in the face of seemingly insurmountable obstacles. I'm especially eager, however, for us to apply this verse not to the great saints of history or even to the contemporary church in general, but to ourselves in particular, the saints that we are by God's grace.

That was one of the many lessons I learned from my friend Clifford. He had a tremendously eternal mind enclosed in a terribly confining body, limited to little movement. His constant struggle against pain and limitation finally ended a few months ago when he died of cancer. I loved Clifford deeply because he deeply understood me. His faith and zeal for evangelism were a constant inspiration to me. He knew so well how to draw his strength from the LORD.

I remember that one day, while pushing his wheelchair through the halls on our way to sing for other patients, I was thinking about what a struggle life was for him. He could barely hold on to my guitar lying on the table of his chair, and it was a great exertion for him to speak and sing. Still he told everyone he met about the great love of his Lord and Savior, Jesus Christ. As we talked that day, he suddenly said, "You know, Marva, life is so wonderful down here, it's hard to imagine that heaven will be even better. But it will be." I was so ashamed. Clifford patiently endured all his sufferings, and he never gave up or grumbled. He never would have uttered the complaints of Isaiah 40:27 (as so often I do). He knew too well the promise of strength in verse 29. His Joy in the LORD overpowered everything else. His heart, mind, and spirit were so eternally fixed that the limitations of his body were surmounted with great struggle and greater Joy.

Clifford always had more than enough strength to carry on his ministry, even in the weakest of times. To a lesser degree, I have understood this verse most clearly at times when I have been called to do specific tasks in ministry for which I have felt inadequate and incapable. At those times, God has accomplished His purposes through me — in spite of me. What is exciting about verse 29 is the realization that we never do really begin to discover the power of God until we learn our own weaknesses.

Although I don't have the space to discuss in detail the theology of weakness inherent in the following comments, the message of God's strength in 2 Corinthians 12:9 is amazing. After Paul besought the Lord to remove his "thorn in the flesh," the Lord answered him, "My grace is sufficient for you, for my power is *brought to its finish* in weakness" (author's translation in italics). The verb that is usually translated "made perfect" in this verse is instead the same verb that Jesus cried from the cross when His work was finished! Every time that verb appears in the New Testament, it is translated "to bring to the finish," with the one exception of 2 Corinthians 12:9. If we brought the customary meaning of that verb to bear on that verse also, we would know more clearly how God's strength is available to us.

What that means for us is that when we are weak, God no longer has to exert His power *on* us. It can be brought to the finish when we are yielded vessels. Then, instead, He can really begin to exert His power *through* us to reach out to others. That is what I saw so profoundly in Clifford. God did not have to exert power on him, for he was an almost perfectly pliable vessel in God's hands. In his weakness, God's power could be brought to its finish. And that is why God's power came *through* Clifford more strongly than almost anyone else I've ever known. "I will glory in my weaknesses then," the apostle Paul concludes literally, "that the power of God may tabernacle upon me." Oh, to have that kind of attitude!

Do we take God up on His promise? Are we able to receive His strength? A friend of mine used to say that we can never know God's power unless we attempt to do something impossible. As long as we are doing things that are within our grasp, things for which we are qualified and capable, we can too easily trust our own strength. Only when we try to do things beyond us will we dependently turn to the LORD and rely solely on Him.

Therefore, a very important part of our church communities should be this claiming of the power of God available to us. We must grasp the visions from Him that allow us to move out boldly in His name and by His strength. Too often, churches wait around until they have the kinds of resources they think they'll need to undertake certain tasks. By the time they begin them, however, it is too often too late, and the ministry is past.

Churches could undertake so much more boldly tasks that they know to be the will of the LORD. We can trust that God will multiply doubly the strengths we need to accomplish His purposes. Most of the churches that are growing today by leaps and bounds are those that move out boldly, creating ministries to match the needs they see, and trusting that God will provide the strength of finances and personnel.

The key to it all lies in knowing the One Who is the Giver and Multiplier of strength. We might be faint or lack the necessary might, but that is irrelevant. In fact, it is better that way, because then God's power can be brought to its finish *on* us and, instead, multiply itself *through* us on behalf of others. We are just "earthen vessels," Paul says in 2 Corinthians 4:7, but in our old clay pots we hold an unspeakable treasure. The fact that we are weak is of great benefit. Then men can see that the transcendent power definitely belongs to God and not to us.

QUESTIONS FOR FURTHER MEDITATION:

1. What forms does the strength of God take when He gives it to me?

2. What have been some particular times when I have been weary and have experienced God's giving me strength?

3. What kinds of things make me weak or destroy my might?

4. How can I use those things to be channels for God's strength rather than sources of bitterness and complaint?

5. How is it true that I never know the power of God until I attempt impossible things?

6. How has the strength the LORD gives to the faint been manifest in my church?

7. In what directions might my church move out more boldly, trusting God to provide the necessary powers and strength?

The Cry of Limitation 30

"Even youths shall faint and be weary,
and young men shall fall exhausted."
Isaiah 40:30

I didn't think the little boy could be real. The son of one of my best friends, he was about four years old at the time. He could run around nonstop, falling, picking himself up again, and charging on into life, from early in the morning until late at night. I couldn't see how his mother could keep up with him. Where did he get all that energy? Yet even he collapsed into bed at night and slept soundly. From the way he expended energy during the day, one would almost get to thinking he would never be tired.

That is the picture Isaiah uses in this verse to compare human beings to the LORD. "Even youths become faint and grow weary," he observes. Both of these terms describing man's weakness and fatigue are identical to the ones asserted in verse 27 to be absent from the character of the LORD. Specifically the opposite is true of man. Even the youth, even those of whom we would least expect it, get tired.

The second line of the couplet is a marvelous example of poetic intensification. Both the subject and the verb from the first line are magnified in these words: "and young men shall fall exhausted." Now the line speaks actually of the firstborn, not in the sense of calling attention to that fact itself, but of stressing its implications: the firstborn are the ones chosen for a double portion, the ones chosen to carry on the family name. In other words, now we are speaking of the cream of the crop. The verb is made more acute by its form; the infinitive absolute actually means "stumbling, they shall stumble." It is the form used in Genesis to indicate the absolute surety of death — "dying, they shall die" — and means here the certainty, the completed action, of the stumbling of those in their prime.

Together these two lines declare, "Even those that we wouldn't expect it of will become faint and grow weary [which never happens to the God of everlastingness], and the very best of those, the cream of the crop, will surely fall." No one can miss Isaiah's point about the inadequacy of man. We think we can get by on our own strength, at least when we're younger, but this verse reminds us that everyone is subject to the same malady. The *New American Standard Bible* uses this intensification: "and vigorous young men stumble badly."

That translation makes me laugh, because I'm an especially uncoordinated stumbler. My cataract-afflicted eyes also contribute some misjudgment of distances, so I trip sometimes over the funniest things. In fact, I broke an arm two years ago when I tripped myself while running and crashed to the pavement. Ridiculous! It helps me to understand, however, that I am also not capable of being as strong as I would like to be spiritually, emotionally, or intellectually.

We are all profoundly deficient and stumble badly spiritually. All of us, no matter our age — even if we are in our prime — must discover sooner or later that we are incapable of having the kind of energy or resources that we need to have to face life and its problems. Even at the times when we seem to be at our greatest, we cannot be good enough to be everything we would want.

Especially we should apply this insight to our attempts to justify our existence, to prove our value and worth to ourselves and the world. We try so hard to be the kind of people that God would want us to be in all our endeavors, but no matter how qualified or how talented we might be, we will stumble and fall. Our nature is inadequate; we are the ones who have corrupted God's perfect design. We would have to be God to avoid the stumbling and falling, and we are not God; nor does it work when we try to make ourselves God.

This verse is especially appropriate now, in the twentieth century, when there is such a lauding of youth. Old people lose out in our culture. They are no longer respected as the wise ones, but are deposited in convalescent centers and left to be lonely. Everyone desires instead to be youthful: we dress in the styles of youth, use the youth language, and fall into the youth fads, all because we think youthfulness is the way to get real "gusto" out of life. We have forgotten that even young men may stumble and fall.

The point of this verse comes from its relation to the preceding and following verses, which teach us that God is the One to give us strength, not we ourselves. God is the Creator of the vim and vigor of our youth, but He goes much further and provides us with His own power and might. Even though youths fail and fall, we shall mount up on eagles' wings, run without weariness, and walk without fainting (see v. 31).

How the world's values are upside down! We think it's best to be young and vigorous and, consequently, get lost in the impetuosity, the superficiality, and the lack of maturity in youth. We seek after the power and strength of youth without recognizing that it is in our weakness, our availability and flexibility to God, that His strength through us is greatest.

Our culture militates against a theology of weakness, for society is built upon seeking after power. We try to exert influence over others; we work hard to establish our reputations; we desire to have our own way. The original sin was just such a longing for power. Contrarily, God would have us learn to be weak. In the truest weakness is seen the truest vision of the grace of God.

This verse emphasizes that our search for strength cannot be a joint effort in which we do our part and need God to do His part to help us. Rather, we must realize that our lives are meaningless without Him, that we need His strength completely to be working through us. We cannot furnish *any* of it on our own. We will become faint and grow weary; we will stumble and fall.

How does this understanding help us in particular moments? It enables us to realize that we don't have to stir up our own strength. I am always amazed that, no matter how tired I am in teaching Bible studies, as soon as I begin to talk about the Word of the LORD, there is a new energy available to me. It's not anything that I can crank up. Much to the contrary, usually I find myself more exhausted before I begin than when my work is finished. Time after time, God's Word is so mighty that it not only carries itself, but it also carries me with it. I wind up with more energy and Joy than before I began to teach. The LORD's strength is refreshing!

God has repeatedly promised that such things will happen, not only because of the efficacy of His Word, but also because of the nature of His power at work within us. Paul praises God so beautifully for this in Ephesians 3:20-21a when he writes, "Now to him who by the power at work within us is able to do far more abundantly than all that we ask or think, to him be glory." *The Living Bible* gives us this exciting paraphrase: "Now glory be to God who by His mighty power at work within us is able to do far more than we would ever dare to ask or even dream of — infinitely beyond our highest prayers, desires, thoughts, or hopes."

Beyond our wildest imaginings — what a promise! Far more abundantly than we could ever experience by ourselves, even in our youth — this is the kind of power that God makes available to us. Because even the best of our youth shall stumble badly, God has a better plan. We do not have to worry if we haven't the strength to complete the tasks to which we are called. God's strength is available to us and readily received. We must begin by knowing we are hopelessly weak.

QUESTIONS FOR FURTHER MEDITATION:

1. How do I see my culture accentuating the glories of youth?
2. What are the inadequacies of youth?
3. How do spiritually young people stumble and fall?
4. How can I help myself and others admit our inadequacies and accept our limitations?
5. How do I claim the power of God to be active in and through my life?
6. What should be the result of my studying verses such as this one?
7. How can the emphasis of this verse by an encouragement for people past their prime who no longer feel useful in life?

The Cry to Wait 31

"But they who wait for the LORD
shall renew their strength,
they shall mount up with wings like eagles,
they shall run and not be weary,
they shall walk and not faint."

Isaiah 40:31

He poured out his soul on the piano. A tremendous burden of guilt had been lifted when he confessed his sin and realized God's forgiveness. His playing was characterized by the power of freedom, and new creative energies were released. After counseling him, I listened from the narthex of the church until suddenly he came running out, asking me to put words to his composition. His music was exquisite! The Lord used it to inspire these words:

The storm is past; The skies grow clear.
Soon all is well   When God is near.

Winds may still toss; Waves crash on shores,
But in God's hands,   The eagle soars!

I shall mount up   On eagle's wings;
I overcome   When my heart sings:

Thanks be to God   For victories
Over my sin.   Forgiveness frees!

The image for our song came from this verse in Isaiah 40. The picture of soaring eagles is one of my favorite expressions of the freedom and strength God gives to those who have become faint and grown weary from the burdens of worry and fear, guilt and sin. Such weightlessness is available to all who wait upon the LORD.

The verse begins with a Hebrew grammatical form that emphasizes the relationship of the LORD with those who wait upon Him.

Actually the phrase reads, "those waiters-upon of the Lord." The form does not necessarily accentuate that they belong to Him (although that is true), but rather that they depend upon Him in a special way.

I traveled a few days ago to Portland to study this verse with my Hebrew professor. On the way to the seminary, I stopped at a Christian bookstore to buy him a present, but the store was not yet open. I had to wait for the clerks to unlock the doors if I wanted to purchase the gift I had in mind. My action couldn't be taken until they acted first.

Similarly, we are "waiters-upon" of the Lord. We look to Him in faith for the fulfillment of His promises to us. We believe in His power and bide our time until He confers His strength. No action can be taken on our part until He has acted first out of the abundance of His grace.

Those who do such waiting, Isaiah promises, "shall renew their strength." The verb actually means "to change it for the better, to substitute it," perhaps even "to exchange it" as one changes garments. In other words, we can turn in our deficient strength and take the Lord's instead. The word translated "strength" is the same one that is the last of four terms in verse 26 and the first of the repetitions in verse 29. Its use again here reminds us of all the things we learned when we meditated upon those verses.

Verse 31 concludes with three pictures of the results from that exchange of strength. First, "they shall mount up on pinions as eagles." The verb is the same one we met in verse 9 and means "to rise or go up," even as the pilgrims went up to the temple, and it is in an imperfect form, which stresses continuous action. We shall continually rise up as we wait upon the Lord.

The word for "pinions" is a fascinating choice. It is derived from a verb that speaks of strength and is related to many words meaning "mighty" or "valiant." The modern Hebrew words for "air force" and "airplane" are derived from the same root. Thus, inherent in the picture of the eagles' wings is an added concept of strength and power.

The last two phrases make use of a poetic device called chiasm, in which two items in sequence are then repeated in reverse order (like a b b a). The two terms "to become faint" and "to grow weary" were used in verse 28 to describe their absence in the God of everlastingness. Then, in verses 29 and 30, they were used to show that man who is the opposite of God possesses them. Now the terms are reversed to emphasize this ending: Those who wait upon the LORD no longer experience growing weary and becoming faint. In addition, the verb is imperfect and shows continuing action. Thus, Isaiah's final point is conclusively made: "They shall run and not be weary; they shall walk and not faint." Period. Exclamation point!

We have seen in the fortieth chapter of Isaiah many important lessons concerning our lives as Christians. Verse 31 seems to bring them all together with seven important concepts. The first four are presented by particular words or phrases; the last three come from the pictures that show what our lives can become when God is in control.

The most important word around which the entire verse focuses is the name LORD. What kind of GOD do we have? We have seen in previous verses many aspects of His character, but we remember especially in connection with the term *Yahweh* that He is a covenant God, a gracious and compassionate God, Who wills the very best for us. Because He is that kind of God, He enables us to wait for Him. We must be "waiters-upon" of Him. We long to deepen our experience of waiting because we believe in Him as LORD of our lives.

The second concept is the waiting itself. We wait eagerly because we know that, in His time and according to His perfect wisdom, the LORD brings all things together for good to those who love Him. We wait restlessly many times, but God would have us learn to wait with perfect trust and confidence. The word *wait* implies absolute realization that the LORD is in control, that in His sovereignty God will accomplish His purposes, which are best for us. Therefore, thinking about the kind of God we have, realizing the immensity of His power and love, and knowing that He alone is the God of everlastingness, we want His perfect plan. We want to want only what He wants. That causes us to depend on Him, to wait for Him, to meditate on His purposes, and, thereby, to act in accordance with His revelation.

What will happen when we wait in such a way? The third

emphasis of this verse is that our strength will be renewed. Not usually associated with this verse, the second meaning of the Hebrew word from which we get "renew" is "to be exchanged." We don't just pep up our own strength; we don't merely supplement it. Rather, we turn it in for that which is new. Our strength as human beings is totally insufficient, and so we have to start all over. In Christ, we start all over with the transformation that makes us new creatures (2 Cor. 5:17).

When we exchange our strength, we don't receive the kind of power the world offers and fights for. We don't receive more blatant might, but we receive, as Paul writes to Timothy in his second letter, "a spirit of power and love and self-control" (1:7). When those three gifts are brought together, we begin to understand the kind of strength God wants us to exert. His strength is modified by love, intelligent and purposeful love directed toward the needs of others, and then further channeled by self-control. This kind of strength reaches out to others and is directed toward their needs, toward the upbuilding and extending of the Kingdom of God.

The kind of strength we receive is the fourth implication we can draw from this verse. When we wait before the LORD, it is not to receive strength only for ourselves. We wait before Him so that His perfect plan can be accomplished for the building up of His Body and the renewing of His Kingdom. We wait to exchange our humanness for God's love, operative through us with all its power. We wait for the renewing of our spirits by the gift of His. We wait to be transformed, to become more and more like the image of His Son, Jesus Christ.

This leads us to the three pictures, three encouraging pictures of the fullness, satisfaction, and completeness of life in the LORD. The first picture is that we shall mount up with pinions like eagles. Perhaps you have watched eagles soaring with such power and grace, always mounting up, gliding with such apparent ease. The picture is glorious. When we wait before the LORD, we, too, shall mount up. Winds may still toss, and waves crash on shores, but in God's hands the eagle soars! The storms of life will continue to buffet us at times, but in the midst of them we can still mount up. God's strength enables us to rise above them. We are as pilgrims in our rising up, ascending the holy hill to worship at the LORD's temple. Having His strength empowers us, in spite of obstacles, to experience His perfect grace. We shall mount up with pinions of strength; we shall be like the eagles in their freedom.

Above all, we shall have a new perspective. The eagle sees from high above the earth. That is the vision offered to us in Ephesians 2:6, where Paul declares that we are "seated with him in the heavenly places in Christ Jesus." Therefore, as he writes to the Colossians, we can "set [our] minds on things that are above" (3:2). By waiting on the LORD, we climb up to view things from His perspective. As we mount up, we are able to get the "big picture." We can see beyond the limits of our present existence into the fact that God has a larger plan, not only for our particular lives, but also a much larger plan for the whole church and for everything by which He will be glorified.

The second picture is that we shall run and not be weary. At first, I found that difficult to comprehend; running tires me out too quickly. However, as I continue to ponder the idea, I realize that other sports for which I have practiced have become quite easy. I could swim for miles. It seems, then, that this picture might imply a bit of training. As we wait before the LORD, He increases our endurance so that more and more we can run and not be weary. What a contrast this is to the previous verse, which warns that even youth shall faint and be weary. Young men shall fall exhausted. Here in verse 31, we have the promise that as we train (in our waiting upon the LORD) we grow in our ability to endure, to continue running without weariness.

The contrast between this picture and the next seems to imply that we have energy for big pushes. We are able to do mighty things, strong things. We can do things for which we are not capable and thereby recognize that it is God indeed Who does them. Running under my own strength, I get very tired. On the other hand, God promises that in His strength, having exchanged ours by waiting before Him, we can do all things — even those for which we are not capable. We can run and not be weary.

The last picture is that we shall walk and not faint. This picture seems to imply steadiness. It suggests consistency of life. The word *walk* is often used in the Scriptures with the connotation of our daily behavior, or course of conduct. As we walk continually in the LORD, we shall not lose the way. We shall not lose heart or become discouraged, but we shall be able to keep on walking.

I always think of mountains when I look at this picture, perhaps because I've wanted for a long time to hike up one, but don't think I have the strength. When I think of walking up a mountain and of the long, steady climb of moving toward the top, I realize that constancy is what's critical. A friend of mine climbed to the top of Mount Rainier for the first time a few weeks ago, and he said that it was necessary to keep moving up constantly, slowly but surely. I want to learn to continue enduring the necessary struggles of daily life and, through it all, to keep on walking consistently in my relationship with the LORD as we move together toward the top.

My friend told me after his return from Mount Rainier of the exhilaration of reaching the top, even in a blizzard, and realizing he had made it. It was very disappointing, then, that immediately, because of the storm, his team had to come back down. The Joy of our walk as Christians is that we are also moving toward the top. We are on our way to meeting the LORD there, face to face. But when we arrive, we won't ever have to come back down. Now it is our purpose to keep on walking and not to faint. It is our exchanged strength that enables us to do that.

Moving on our way toward heaven through this life, we realize that when we get to the top, we are there to stay. That implies a crucial assurance. Because it is so difficult to keep going sometimes, it is most helpful to know that we will indeed make it by God's grace. When this picture promises us that we shall walk and not faint, it implies that our walking can be characterized by the sure knowledge that we will indeed make it. We shall continue to walk, and we will not faint. We know we can overcome all obstacles because God has begun His work in our lives, and He has promised to bring that work to completion until the day of Jesus Christ (Phil. 1:6).

We shall walk and not faint because we wait upon the LORD. We have exchanged our feeble strength for His own; we are filled with His Spirit for the walking. We move toward the goal of the upward call of God in Jesus Christ (Phil. 3:14), and toward the time of knowing the LORD face to face. Ultimately, that is what we wait for, and while we wait we move. While we wait, we live in a world that needs to know the Truth about our waiting.

QUESTIONS FOR FURTHER MEDITATION:

1. What obstacles in my life frustrate my waiting?

2. What kinds of doubts do I have about the character of the LORD?

3. Why is it so hard for me to trust God's perfect goodness and thereby to wait for His timing?

4. What might be the problem in those moments when I don't realize the strength of the LORD in my life?

5. How can the promise of this verse motivate me in difficult times?

6. How does this verse give me promises related to other truths I have learned from Isaiah 40?

7. How has this chapter from Isaiah changed my life as I have studied it?